A
$AVING
FAITH

A $aving Faith

A New Look at a Disciple's Finances

EDITED BY
DECLAN JOYCE

INTRODUCTION BY
STEVE JOHNSON

DPI

DISCIPLESHIP
PUBLICATIONS
INTERNATIONAL

IMPORTANT CAUTION: PLEASE READ THIS!

Readers are strongly encouraged to consult with a financial planning professional or financial advisers before adopting the guidelines in this book. Each individual is responsible to adapt these guidelines to their specific needs and situations.

This book is based on information from sources believed to be reliable, and every effort has been made to make the book accurate and complete, based on the information available as of the printing date, but its accuracy and completeness are not guaranteed. Despite the best efforts and intentions of the authors and publishers, the book may contain mistakes, and the reader should use the book only as a general guide and not as the ultimate source of advice or information about the subject of this book.

The book is not intended to represent a definitive source of information on the subject of personal finances, but rather to simplify, complement and supplement other available sources. The reader is encouraged to read all available material and to seek professional advice in order to learn as much as possible about this subject.

The authors and publisher are not engaged in rendering financial advice, nor do they represent that they are financial experts. If the reader desires financial advice, he should seek the services of a competent financial expert.

This book is sold without warranties of any kind, express or implied, and the publisher and author disclaim any liability, loss or damage caused by the contents of this book. Any loss or damage incurred is the sole responsibility of the reader and is the result of the reader's own decisions.

If you do not wish to be bound by the foregoing cautions and conditions, you may return the book to the publisher for a full refund.

Publisher's Note

In the spring of 1998 Steve Johnson, the lead evangelist for the New York City Church of Christ, organized a seminar designed to help the members of that congregation see that personal management is definitely a spiritual issue.

Steve felt strongly that disciples have often looked at their finances from only one perspective. Therefore, he wished to bring together Christians who could teach on this subject in such a way as to give those who follow Jesus a broader understanding of the role finances should play in their lives. Following that weekend seminar, Steve had members of his staff transcribe the lessons that had been presented. Those lessons were then edited by Declan Joyce, a talented disciple in the NYC church, who submitted them back to the authors for additional changes. After some final edits by our staff at DPI, we are proud to present this volume which should help Christians, especially in Western countries, handle their finances in ways that bring greater honor to God.

Contents

Jesus Saves...
and So Should You

by Steve Johnson

What we are attempting to do in this book is something that to my knowledge has never been done in our churches before. In the past most of the financial workshops that we have conducted have been given from the viewpoint of contributing more money to God and his church. I am all for that, of course, and I would never discourage anyone from giving all they can to God. But in this book we want to talk about a subject that I think many Christians are uncomfortable discussing: *making and saving money*. Deep down, a lot of us feel that it is somehow unspiritual to be concerned with such matters. But while it is true that the Bible condemns being overly concerned with money, it does not condemn making it. Some of us, in a good-hearted attempt to free ourselves from worldly concerns, have gone too far to the other extreme and now find ourselves in debt, unable to help other people and unable to contribute regularly and sacrificially to the needs of the church. Many of us are enslaved to credit card companies and other lenders. We are enslaved to interest rates of 19 and 21 percent, and until we extricate ourselves from the mess we have gotten into, we are going to be seriously hampered in our ability to make our lives attractive to others.

> *We have different gifts, according to the grace given us. If a man's gift is prophesying, let him use it in proportion to his faith. If it is serving, let him serve; if it is teaching, let him teach; if it is encouraging, let him encourage; if it is contributing to the needs of others, let him give generously; if it is*

leadership, let him govern diligently; if it is showing mercy, let
him do it cheerfully. (Romans 12:6-8)

The part of this passage I want to focus on is "if it is contributing to the needs of others, let him do it generously." In order to
have the gift of giving, you have to have the gift of *making*. I
remember, during my rebellious teen years, having a conversation with my dad about being responsible with money. At the
time I wanted to be a hippie, and I considered all material things
to be innately bad. But my dad knew that I wanted to be a Christian, so he asked me, "How are you going to feel if someone who
is less well off than you comes to you looking for help, and you
are unable to help them?" My dad was wise enough to know that
if he approached the topic from that angle, he would get through
to me. He knew that I considered being able to help others an
important part of discipleship. Likewise, all of us as disciples are
in the same position. If our finances are a mess, what are we
going to do when someone comes to us in genuine need?

> *But whatever was to my profit I now consider loss for the sake*
> *of Christ. What is more, I consider everything a loss compared*
> *to the surpassing greatness of knowing Christ Jesus my Lord,*
> *for whose sake I have lost all things. I consider them rubbish,*
> *that I may gain Christ and be found in him, not having a righ-*
> *teousness of my own that comes from the law, but that which is*
> *through faith in Christ—the righteousness that comes from God*
> *and is by faith. (Philippians 3:7-9)*

Paul truly considered all things to be rubbish compared to
knowing Christ: his education (he was educated by the famous
Gamaliel), his lineage, his birthright, his Roman citizenship. Similarly, many of us consider all the things of this world (education,
money, etc.) to be rubbish. But they are not rubbish. They are
rubbish compared to knowing Christ, but in and of themselves

they are not rubbish. In Acts 22:25, Paul is about to be flogged, and he asks the centurion, "Is it legal for you to flog a Roman citizen who hasn't even been found guilty?" They back off when they realize he is a citizen, and Paul escapes a beating. In other words, he considered his citizenship rubbish compared to knowing Christ, but not compared to a beating. And that is the way it ought to be with all of us.

In Mark 10 the rich young ruler comes to Jesus and asks what he must do to inherit eternal life. As most of you know, Jesus tells him that he must sell everything he has. At this the ruler walks away, unwilling to do so. Some of us take this passage to mean that as disciples we must get rid of all our material goods in order to follow Jesus, and in a sense this is true. But look at what Jesus says just a few verses later:

> *"I tell you the truth," Jesus replied, "no one who has left home or brothers or sisters or mother or father or children or fields for me and the gospel will fail to receive a hundred times as much in this present age (homes, brothers, sisters, mothers, children and fields—and with them, persecutions) and in the age to come, eternal life." (Mark 10:29-30)*

In this passage, Jesus specifically mentions things that some of us feel that we ought not to aspire to attain. He says yes, you must give up everything to be my disciple, but part of the result of living a faithful and righteous life is receiving things back in this life. So the idea that some of us have that it is wrong to attain material things is really an un-Biblical idea.

> *"For I know the plans I have for you," declares the LORD, "plans to prosper you and not to harm you, plans to give you hope and a future." (Jeremiah 29:11)*

The Lord and prosperity go hand in hand. The Bible is full of examples of God wanting to make his people prosperous, just as it is full of stories of God's people *not* prospering when they disobey him. In the last chapter of the book of Job, we find that Job, having been tested and persecuted by Satan, receives back everything that he had lost, and much more besides:

The Lord blessed the latter part of Job's life more than the first. He had fourteen thousand sheep, six thousand camels, a thousand yoke of oxen and a thousand donkeys. And he also had seven sons and daughters.... Nowhere in all the land were there found women as beautiful as Job's daughters, and their father granted them an inheritance along with their brothers. (Job 42:12-15)

I believe scriptures such as these should be as important in the lives of disciples as the scriptures that tell us to be evangelistic, to share our faith and to be fruitful. Consider two more:

Make it your ambition to lead a quiet life, to mind your own business and to work with your hands, just as we told you, so that your daily life may win the respect of outsiders and so that you will not be dependent on anybody. (1 Thessalonians 4:11-12)

And we urge you, brothers, warn those who are idle, encourage the timid, help the weak, be patient with everyone. (1 Thessalonians 5:14)

I would venture to say that many of us are not fruitful because we have yet to make these scriptures a part of our lives. We have not yet learned the difference between minding our business and sharing our faith.

Both letters to the Thessalonians were written to people who believed that Jesus was coming back imminently. As a result, many of the Thessalonian disciples had quit their jobs and were sitting around waiting for the Lord to return. This is why Paul says in 2 Thessalonians that no one knows for sure when

Jesus will be returning and that it is therefore necessary for Christians to be working. He is, in fact, extremely emphatic about it. Consider these passages:

In the name of the Lord Jesus Christ, we command you, brothers, to keep away from every brother who is idle and who does not live according to the teaching you received from us. (2 Thessalonians 3:6)

If anyone does not obey our instruction in this letter, take special note of him. Do not associate with him, in order that he may feel ashamed. Yet do not regard him as an enemy, but warn him as a brother. (2 Thessalonians 3:14-15)

If anyone does not provide for his relatives, and especially for his immediate family, he has denied the faith and is worse than an unbeliever. (1 Timothy 5:8)

It is hard to imagine Paul being more emphatic on the subject of living a responsible financial life. Now consider this passage:

But godliness with contentment is great gain. For we brought nothing into the world, and we can take nothing out of it. But if we have food and clothing, we will be content with that. People who want to get rich fall into temptation and a trap and into many foolish and harmful desires that plunge men into ruin and destruction. For the love of money is a root of all kinds of evil. Some people, eager for money, have wandered from the faith and pierced themselves with many griefs. (1 Timothy 6:6-10)

Again, this is a passage that causes confusion with many disciples. You need to understand that there is a very substantial difference between wanting to prosper by earning a good living to support your family and just wanting to get rich for the sake of getting rich. Money, despite what the old saw says, is not the root of all evil. Paul says that "the *love* of money is a root of all kinds of evil." Money is an inanimate object. It is not inherently evil. There are a number of things, money included, that can be obstacles to us becoming disciples, and yet we do not get rid of them. Marriage, for example, can be an obstacle if the spouse is actively opposed to the church. Yet the Bible does not give anyone license to leave that person for that reason. God esteems marriage greatly and commands that it be respected. Similarly, money is capable of leading someone down a path away from discipleship, but it is not inherently evil. Money is just a thing; our spiritual attitude toward it is what can ultimately lead us to succeed or to sin with it. If we are in a situation in which all we have is "food and clothing" and for whatever reason we are unable to have more, then we should indeed be content with that. But again, we are not forbidden from pursuing more, as long as we are careful to place spiritual priorities first. Before I close this introduction, let me talk about saving three things.

Saving Our Reputations

Time and time again I've found that some of us, through our own insecurity and pride, have held other disciples back who are very focused on their careers. I had a conversation recently with a brother who is a bank president with Citicorp in Chicago, and we were discussing some of the issues that we hoped to cover in this book. He was very thankful to be able to talk, and he said to me, "Steve, I've lost count of the number of times I've been discouraged by my brothers and sisters from being a bank president and how many times people have tried to get me to do something else—or just felt that my job was not a spiritual endeavor." I think it's sad that anyone would feel this way about their career.

We need disciples in all walks of life, and we need them to be excellent in their jobs, whatever they may be. Do not let insecurity motivate you to drag down your brothers and sisters who are being wholehearted in pursuing their careers. Take a look at this passage:

> *Teach slaves to be subject to their masters in everything, to try to please them, not to talk back to them, and not to steal from them, but to show that they can be fully trusted, so that in every way they will make the teaching about God our Savior attractive. (Titus 2:9-10)*

If slaves were told that they could make the teaching about Christ attractive, how much more should we in our careers? This is, I believe, an indication of how much we should be focused on making our careers excellent. Work performance is a spiritual issue.

Saving Our Money

It is the personal responsibility of each one of us to be excellent in our finances—not just paying all our bills on time but having a correct spiritual attitude about money. Let me warn you about two traps: envy and greed. Envy is a sin. You cannot be envious of those who are financially better off than you are. This is not going to help you to get on top of your financial planning. If you know someone in the church who has been successful in his or her career, do not let that embitter you. Instead, be smart and ask for their advice.

On the other hand, if you have been materially blessed, do not be greedy. The Bible commands the rich to be generous. Whatever category you currently find yourself in, strive to become someone who is in a position to help others. I believe, for example, that we have a responsibility to help the poor. If you look in the book of Acts, you will see that time and time again the poor who were helped were members of the church. We have an opportunity to see to it that, in our lifetimes, there will be no such thing as a homeless disciple anywhere in the world. This will not happen, however, if we do not have a spiritual attitude about our finances.

Saving Souls

Saving souls, as always, is the bottom line. The Bible makes it clear that how we handle our finances is a spiritual issue, and I believe that any spiritual issue that we are willing to deal with is ultimately going to make us better disciples. Examine your attitudes about prosperity and financial matters. Are they in line with what the Bible teaches?

In the remainder of this book, you will receive the kind of advice for which people pay thousands of dollars. It will be of little value to you, however, if your mind is not set on pleasing God with your career and finances. I pray that the issues covered herein will inspire you to become not only responsible with money but better equipped to fulfill God's purposes for your life. Remember, Jesus saves...and so should you.

Finances:
A Spiritual Issue

BY JIM BROWN

I have good news about getting out of debt and getting on top of your finances, and good news about getting back hope and a future.

> *"For I know the plans I have for you," declares the LORD, "plans to prosper you and not to harm you, plans to give you hope and a future." (Jeremiah 29:11)*

This is what God wants for each one of us. He wants us to prosper in every way as disciples. He wants us to be effective in everything we do, so that everything we are a part of will make an eternal difference, either in our own lives or in the lives of others. Finances are an integral part of our spiritual lives. You can say to yourself, "I just hope my problems with debt will go away," but they will not just disappear by wishing. You can say, "I don't want to think about it," but you *need* to think about it!

What qualifies me to write on debt management? First, I am a disciple. Second, I have a background in finances. Third and most important, I am debt free. This is what qualifies me to teach.

You Must Have Finances

The most basic requirement for your finances is, obviously, that you must have some! You have to have money in order to have a workable budget. In 2 Thessalonians 3:6-8a the apostle Paul writes,

> *In the name of the Lord Jesus Christ, we command you, brothers, to keep away from every brother who is idle and does not live according to the teaching you received from us. For you yourselves know how you ought to follow our example. We were not idle when we were with you, nor did we eat anyone's food without paying for it.*

Have you ever opened up a refrigerator at a brother's or sister's house and just helped yourself? It seems that Paul would have a problem with that. Instead, he "worked night and day, laboring and toiling so that [he] would not be a burden to [anyone]" (2 Thessalonians 3:8b). Also, Paul did not borrow money from any of the brothers; he had his own. He goes on to say,

> *We did this, not because we do not have the right to such help, but in order to make ourselves a model for you to follow. For even when we were with you, we gave you this rule: "If a man will not work, he shall not eat." (2 Thessalonians 3:9-10)*

That's quite a rule! He continues,

> *We hear that some among you are idle. They are not busy; they are busybodies. Such people we command and urge in the Lord Jesus Christ to settle down and earn the bread they eat. And as for you brothers, never tire of doing what is right. (2 Thessalonians 3:11-13)*

Now look at the next part:

> *If anyone does not obey our instruction in this letter, take special note of him. Do not associate with him, in order that he*

*may feel ashamed. Yet do not regard him as an enemy, but warn
him as a brother. (2 Thessalonians 3: 14-15)*

Paul is saying that brothers (or sisters) who do not work
need to be warned. If they refuse to work, you cannot even associate with them. We are not to regard them as enemies, but we
must be honest and direct with them as brothers. The Bible is
very emphatic about the need for every disciple to work and to
support themselves. We need to have money and for most of us,
the only way to do that is to get a job. Some of us have jobs, but
they are jobs that are going nowhere. I realize that there are
times that we just need to get a "survival job," but for a lot of us
it is time to get a degree, or to go back to school to finish a
degree—so that you can get a better job.

Once you have a job, you have to do it well. In Colossians
3:23-24 Paul writes:

*Whatever you do, work at it with all your heart, as working for
the Lord, not for men, since you know that you will receive an
inheritance from the Lord as a reward. It is the Lord Christ you
are serving.*

The Bible makes it clear that job performance is a spiritual issue.
It is a test of your discipleship. We need to treat our bosses the
way we would treat Jesus Christ. If Jesus were your boss, how
would your job performance be different? I am sure that you
would work through lunch if necessary and you would stay late,
if that were required. You would do whatever was necessary to be
exemplary. You would love your job, and you would be eager
about it. Guess what? This is exactly how you need to be with
your earthly boss. Otherwise, how are you going to win him
(and your other coworkers) for Christ? Thus, your job is a test of
your Christianity; it *is* a spiritual issue.

When you are a great employee, bosses will usually bend over backward to help you because they do not want you to leave. I hear disciples say, "I have to work during church services on Sunday or I'll get fired from my job." Let me tell you something: If you are the type of employee that you need to be—getting there early, staying late if need be, bright-eyed and bushy-tailed and always having a good attitude—and you say, "Look, I just can't work on Sundays or during my midweek service," most of the time your boss will work it out for you. He knows that it is in his best interest to do so because you do not steal or cheat and you are great with customers. Why would he want to lose you?

A few of us are probably feeling a little heavy, thinking, *I don't have a job so no one is going to associate with me now!* Well, I have great news for you! I have a job for you. It starts Monday morning at 8:00 and ends that day at 5:00 pm or later. You will get paid nothing. I know you are wondering what kind of a job this is.... It is the job of looking for a job. You are now fully employed as a job hunter. If you are single, when your roommates leave the apartment for their jobs at 7:00 am, so do you. When they come home at 6:00 or 7:00 after a long day's work, so do you. When they talk about how challenging their day was, you're right there with them. So, now you have a job and you can eat and associate with the body of believers. You are all united.

If you are out there looking for a job from 8:00 am to 5:00 pm every day, God will bless you. My wife, Teresa, told me that every time she was in that situation, three days did not go by before she found a job. You may not land your dream job at first—just get any job—because the bosses at the really good jobs are always going to ask, "Where are you working now?" They want to hire someone who is already working.

You Must Be
Financially Responsible

"Whoever can be trusted with very little can also be trusted with much, and whoever is dishonest with very little will also be dishonest with much. So if you have not been trustworthy in handling worldly wealth, who will trust you with true riches? And if you have not been trustworthy with someone else's property, who will give you property of your own?" (Luke 16:10-12)

In this passage, God is equating the manner in which you handle money with your spiritual life. If you are not a good manager of your money, you cannot be a good manager in the kingdom. God cannot give you all the spiritual riches he longs to give you if you have not first proven that you are responsible with the money with which he has blessed you. The way you handle your money is a test of your heart for discipleship, your faithfulness to God, and your readiness to be trusted with someone's soul. Let's look at four areas in which we need to prove our trust to God.

NEVER CHEAT GOD

"Will a man rob God? Yet you rob me.
"But you ask, 'How do we rob you?'
"In tithes and offerings. You are under a curse—the whole nation of you—because you are robbing me. Bring the whole tithe into the storehouse, that there may be food in my house. Test me in this," says the Lord Almighty, "and see if I will not throw open the floodgates of heaven and pour out so much blessing that you will not have enough room for it. I will prevent pests from devouring your crops, and the vines in your fields will not cast their fruit," says the Lord Almighty. "Then all the nations will call you blessed, for yours will be a delightful land," says the Lord Almighty. (Malachi 3:8-12)

God's point? Don't cheat him. Bring in the whole tithe and the whole offering.

> *"When you bring injured, crippled or diseased animals and offer them as sacrifices, should I accept them from your hands?" says the Lord. "Cursed is the cheat who has an acceptable male in his flock and vows to give it, but then sacrifices a blemished animal to the Lord. For I am a great king," says the Lord Almighty, "and my name is to be feared among the nations."* (Malachi 1:13b-14)

If you cheat God, do not expect a whole lot of blessings from him. If you want to get on top of your finances and enjoy the prosperity that he brings, then you cannot cheat God. He says that you are "cursed" if you vow to give your best to him and then renege. When we became disciples, we vowed to give our best to him, our firstfruits. In other words, a tithe of our gross salary. (There is a big difference between "gross" and "net earnings." We tithe from the gross. After the government takes their cut, it is called the "net.") In the first world churches, we also commit to a yearly missions contribution to plant churches. Typically, a disciple will give about 15 percent of his gross income to God. If you think that seems like a lot, consider a Jew in Jesus' time. Ten percent of his income went as a tithe to the Levites. Another 10 percent went for feasts. Additionally, every three years he gave 10 percent of his income to the destitute. This totals more than 23 percent on tithes alone. On top of that, they had offerings: wave offerings, freewill offerings, guilt offerings, thanksgiving offerings and special offerings. Then the Romans would come in and tax them heavily. So what did that leave? Not much.

> *Now this is what the Lord Almighty says: "Give careful thought to your ways. You have planted much, but have harvested little. You eat, but never have enough. You drink, but never have your*

fill. You put on clothes, but are not warm. You earn wages, only to put them in a purse with holes in it." (Haggai 1:5-6)

Have you ever felt like you never have money? All of us can relate to that. Haggai is saying that one of the reasons that this happens is because we cheat God. We think we need some or all of the money that we had previously committed to him so we hold back on giving to him. If you give to God first, you will find that God sews up those holes in your pocket! When you are really on track, you will have money and think, *Where did that come from?*

TAKE CARE OF YOUR HOUSEHOLD

If anyone does not provide for his relatives, and especially for his immediate family, he has denied the faith and is worse than an unbeliever. (1 Timothy 5:8)

This is a strong teaching. How do you measure up? Husbands: Do you just go to the automatic teller machine (ATM), take out some cash and put it in your pocket without your wife knowing anything about it? That is not right. Wives: Do you go on little shopping sprees without anyone knowing what you bought? That is not right either. Husbands and wives need to be open with one another and communicate about money regularly. Work a discussion of finances into your weekly scheduling time. Discuss purchases with one another. One solution is to have a rule where one partner cannot make any nonessential purchases above a certain amount without the consent of the other. I have seen husbands spend money on compact discs (CDs) and sporting equipment while their wives were have trouble putting food on the table. Living like this, how are you going to get your kids through college? Get on top of your finances, and start saving right now.

How about retirement? Even though we need to be living every day of our lives spiritually as if it were our last, as good stewards of our money, we need to prepare for the future in a righteous way. However, do not hold back on your contribution so you can save for these reasons. Honor God first, than take care of the future.

If you do not have a checking account, you need one. You get a great tax deduction from the government for your contribution to the church and other charitable contributions, and canceled checks are your best way to document these contributions. When I was eleven years old, my Dad gave me $100 to open up my own checking account. He told me that if I bounced a check, he would take it all back. At eleven years old, back in 1968, $100 was major wealth! So I never bounced a check. It was tough writing checks at eleven years old: Not many people wanted to take them! Everyone wanted to see some identification, and at eleven you do not have any ID! But I did manage to write some checks and kept close track of the money I had left. It taught me to be a good steward of my finances. Parents, it would not be a bad idea to consider something similar for your children.

LOVE THE BROTHERS

Let no debt remain outstanding, except the continuing debt to love one another. (Romans 13:8a)

In many cases, disciples' financial management is so poor that they frequently run out of money and have to borrow from their brothers and sisters. It shows a gross lack of discipline, and as we have seen from the Scriptures, if God cannot trust you with money, how can he trust you with souls? I strongly, strongly discourage any borrowing or lending of money between disciples. I realize that there are genuine emergencies when we lend without even expecting repayment. I do not mean situations like this. I mean facing the fact that you messed up and now living with it—without borrowing. For example you may need to scrounge and eat the rice that has been at the bottom of the refrigerator for two weeks, or the pasta in the back of the cupboard, or the sack of dried black beans left over from a gag gift. With that kind of righteous attitude, God will sew up the holes in your pockets, you will get on top of your finances, and you will be on your way to being a success story.

HATE DEBT

Financially speaking, there are two types of people: those who get ahead and those who fall behind. The difference between the two is debt. Those who get into debt fall way behind; those who have no debt get ahead. It is as simple as that!

Of course, there is such a thing as a responsible and acceptable debt, like a student loan. However, to get student loans and then not finish a degree should not be viewed as acceptable. To go into debt for school and then have nothing to show for it is foolish.

A business loan is an acceptable debt, provided the plan for your business is a thorough and realistic one. A house mortgage is acceptable debt, as long as it is within your budget and can be paid off in a reasonable amount of time. A car loan is a little less clear. It is better to buy a used car that you can afford than to buy a new one for which you cannot afford to make the payments. New cars are considered by many finance professionals to be one of the world's worst investment choices because of how much depreciation occurs during the early life of the vehicle. (And keep in mind that leases, which are growing in popularity, are just another form of debt.)

Now let's look at debt that is just plain bad: The number one offender is credit cards with unpaid balances. Oh, that golden plastic moment! Swish, swish. It makes some feel so good to hand over that credit card to get what they want—until they get the bill! Credit cards are not bad in and of themselves, but you should make it your goal to never carry a balance. My conviction is so strong about this that I have four credit cards, and I have never carried a balance on any of them. I have never paid a finance charge, and I have never paid a late fee. Credit card companies hate me. They make billions and billions of dollars on the finance charges and late fees charged to the financially undisciplined. They love people who carry balances. They send such people more credit cards. They tell these people they are preapproved! They say, "Your excellent record has 'gained' you a platinum card!" Or maybe it's a super-mega-ultra platinum card! The credit card companies try to make us feel like not accepting their offer makes us idiots. I just take all those offers and throw them into the trash where they belong!

If you get into credit card debt, you become a slave. You feel like a slave. You get discouraged and depressed. Those of you who are in credit card debt need to get out as quickly as possible. Some of us are paying 18 to 20 percent interest or more. You are being eaten alive financially and you need to get out of credit card debt and never, ever get into it again. Many people come into the kingdom with a load of credit card debt. Some who have been in the kingdom a long time have also been sucked into this trap. Many with that kind of debt live in denial. There will be more advice in this book about what to do, but just don't stay in denial. Open up with someone who will help you work out a plan to get that debt off your back.

One time I was going through my family's ranch house in Montana when I saw a ball of string which my great-aunt, who is in her 90s, had made. She had made it years earlier, during the Great Depression. It was not an ordinary ball of string. It consisted of many small lengths of string tied together. She had carefully made a square knot at the end of each length and rolled them up into a single ball. I looked at that and thought, *I would never do that.* Then I thought, *That's the problem. I would never do that.* This is precisely how we need to be with our money, carefully knotting it together, a little at a time. I call it a "Great Depression Bunch of String."

Many older Americans have very fond memories of the Great Depression when they were forced to make do with a little. It gave them good habits that have lasted them a lifetime. It has been proven that most millionaires in America are not large salary earners or people who have inherited money. They are people with good financial habits who have put their money together a little at a time (see Proverbs 13:11). A penny saved is a penny earned. A hundred dollars not spent is a hundred dollars in savings.

> *Jesus told his disciples: "There was a rich man whose manager was accused of wasting his possessions. So he called him in and asked him, 'What is this I hear about you? Give an account of your management, because you cannot be manager any longer.'*
>
> *"The manager said to himself, 'What shall I do now? My master is taking away my job. I'm not strong enough to dig, and I'm ashamed to beg—I know what I'll do so that, when I lose my job here, people will welcome me into their houses.'*
>
> *"So he called in each one of his master's debtors. He asked the first, 'How much do you owe my master?'*
>
> *"'Eight hundred gallons of olive oil,' he replied.*
>
> *"The manager told him, 'Take your bill, sit down quickly, and make it four hundred.'*

"Then he asked the second, 'And how much do you owe?'
"'A thousand bushels of wheat,' he replied.
"He told him, 'Take your bill and make it eight hundred.'
"The master commended the dishonest manager because
he had acted shrewdly. For the people of this world are more
shrewd in dealing with their own kind than are the people of the
light. I tell you, use worldly wealth to gain friends for your-
selves, so that when it is gone, you will be welcomed into eter-
nal dwellings." (Luke 16:1-9)

It is a godly trait to be shrewd with our finances. It is a worldly attitude to spend money however we want to, and then get jealous of those who have money left to spend. We can even accuse people who are on top of their finances and who have money to spare of being worldly. This is not right!

We need to be shrewd spiritual men and women who strive for greatness in our finances. We need to use our money and possessions to advance the kingdom. A good rule of thumb is to give according to your income and live as if you only made half of it. Remember that no matter how much debt you are carrying, you can conquer it with the power of God (Matthew 19:26). Be hopeful, be excited, and never give up! You will be victorious!

Realizing Your
Financial Dreams

BY GREG GARCIA

*It is for freedom that Christ has set us free....You, my broth-
ers, were called to be free. But do not use your freedom to
indulge the sinful nature; rather, serve one another in love.
(Galatians 5:1, 13)*

*Those who live according to the sinful nature have their minds
set on what that nature desires; but those who live in accordance with the Spirit have their minds set on what the Spirit
desires. (Romans 8:5)*

I want to show you the path to freedom. I want you to be
free to live wherever you want, free to drive whatever you want,
free to do what you want with your life—and free to do awesome
things for God! This is not the path to getting rich quick or the
path of "prosperity theology" ladled out by televangelists. Nor
am I encouraging you to live a selfish life of indulgence. I am
talking about a solid, scriptural way to financially attain the kind
of life that I believe God wants us all to enjoy.

Money has great spiritual power for good or ill. Two-thirds
of all the parables in the Bible talk about it. However, a lot of us
have not taken these parables to heart. We are in fact enslaved

today to bad financial habits. Many of us came into the kingdom with bad habits, and many still have them. We are "spenders" rather than "savers"; we carry credit card balances; and we look at everything in terms of "How much is the monthly payment?" As long as we continue to operate this way, we will continue to be enslaved and we will never be in a position to help others.

What should your ultimate financial goal be? Here is a definition that I came up with and on which I have gotten a lot of good feedback. I define financial freedom as follows: *To live in the home you want and enjoy the lifestyle you believe fits with your discipleship, completely debt-free, with enough invested to generate what you need to maintain that lifestyle, all the while honoring God with the firstfruits of what he has given you, and growing in your generosity.*

God wants you to have the desires of your heart (Psalm 37:4). Do you believe this? Most of us say we do, but we do not live as if we believe it. We really do not trust that God cares about our careers or our living situations or our kids. As a young Christian, I had a hard time believing it myself. I believed that every time I messed up spiritually in any way, God was mad. I felt like he had a big register, and he was keeping close tabs on me. I finally figured out that there was something wrong with me, not with God. I would look around and see disciples who were fruitful, effective and happy, and I knew that I just was not getting it. Finally, it dawned on me that if God loved me when I was living a completely sinful life, never giving him a second thought, then surely he loves me now that I love him and am trying, however imperfectly, to please him.

In John 10:10 Jesus says that he has come to give us life to the full. What exactly is "life to the full"? It means abundant fruitfulness and righteousness, to be sure, but I think it means more than that. God wants for you to have the absolute best, an abundant life in every way. God is generous and giving. Did you ever notice that when you pray to him for something specific, he gives you more than you asked for? God always gives us more than we ask for, not just the bare minimum (Malachi 3:10b). Because of this, when it comes to a special missions contribution or any other financial need that the church has, I always make a point of going beyond what is asked. The Bible says that the Roman centurion amazed Jesus with his faith. I want to try to amaze God with my faith and generosity, just as he consistently amazes me.

> *Then Jesus declared, "I am the bread of life. He who comes to me will never go hungry, and he who believes in me will never be thirsty." (John 6:35)*

Do you think Jesus is talking just about food and water? I believe he is talking about every area of life: material, physical and spiritual. I am completely satisfied today in every way. My marriage to my wife, Kay, is a good example of this. We have been married 19 years, and our marriage just gets better every year, as we have been discipled and helped in various areas. I am completely satisfied in my marriage. I am not hungry or thirsty for anyone else. This is what John 6:35 means to me: being satisfied in every aspect of my life. We first need to believe that this is what God wants for us and then our faith can grow from there.

Step One:
Be Generous

> *"Give, and it will be given to you. A good measure, pressed down, shaken together and running over, will be poured into your lap. For with the measure you use, it will be measured to you." (Luke 6:38)*

God's generosity to us demands that we respond in kind. There was a time when I did not have this on straight. But that changed June 30, 1992, a real spiritual milestone for me. Steve and Kim Sapp, the leaders of the Atlanta church, and Don and Leigh Burroughs, also on the ministry staff, asked my wife and me to come over for the evening. I thought we would be talking about the summer plans for the ministry. It turned out, however, the agenda was me.

At the time we had three nice cars: a Mercedes convertible, a Volvo station wagon and a Saab convertible. The Mercedes was my business car, the Volvo was for family outings, and the Saab was my wife's car. I thought this was fine. You know, I was giving plenty to the church, more than a tithe, so in my mind everything was fine. Steve basically said to me, "I need to talk to you about money. I'm not trying to get you to give more to the church. But you have three nice cars, you do all this work on your house, you have this great ability to make money, but you are just not known as a generous person. People do not feel blessed from being around you. I'm not even asking you to sell one of your cars. But I want you to think about being creative in your giving, and working on becoming known as a generous person."

Now, I have two great fears in life. One is sexual sin. I take every precaution in this area. I watch hardly any television; I do not watch movies that have any nudity; I never have lunch alone with any woman who is not my wife, my mother or my daughter. I know I am not beyond falling into sin in this area, and I am afraid of it. The second sin is greed, which in a way I am more afraid of because it is more insidious. Money and acquisitiveness can very easily become a preoccupation and get a grip on the heart. In the Parable of the Sower, Jesus talks about four types of soil. Most of us who have been in the kingdom for a while are not the first or second type of soil. But we will never know whether we are the third or fourth kind of soil until the day we die. Weeds are constantly trying to clog up our hearts. Steve Sapp did me a very great favor on that night in 1992 when he tore some weeds out of my heart that posed a very real spiritual threat to me. That conversation went on for two hours, and it hurt. I felt so much insecurity and pain, but I followed my own personal rule for discipling, which is to shut up and listen.

After the first two hours were over, I spent another two hours alone with Steve and Don to get some more practical advice on what to do. Then I went home and prayed for an hour and a half. It was 3:00 am when I went to bed after having made some serious decisions. For starters I decided that night that I was going to become a generous person: generous with my employees, with people who work on my house, with brothers and sisters, with birthdays and with special occasions. My wife is naturally a generous person, and I had always tended to hold her back. I decided to change that. As a result, I began to do things anonymously: I gave to people who were in need and requested that they not tell anybody about it because I did not want any credit for it. I just wanted to become someone for whom generosity was second nature. In other words I wanted to become more like God.

The day after the meeting with Steve and Don, I gave an employee of someone working on my house a check for $50. "Here," I said, "don't tell your boss. This is for you." The day after that I had a client come in from St. Louis, and I gave him his bill for a tax return I had prepared for him. He had a very complicated tax return and his bill was $2700. He amazed me by telling me to add $800 to it because he didn't think I had charged him enough and because his employer was reimbursing him for this expense! This is the way God operates: He is infinitely more generous with us when we ourselves are being generous.

Since that night in 1992, I have really stuck to the commitment I made, and beginning that very year, my income grew by more than 35 percent! It has continued to steadily increase every year since. I have striven to become a generous person, and I want to urge you to do likewise. This is a vital step in becoming financially independent as a disciple. Do not just give your tithe or your special missions contribution, calling it generosity. Become a naturally generous person. Make it something for which you are known.

Let me add two caveats. First, if your own financial house is not in order, and if you have serious problems with debt, you should certainly get advice about how to be generous in those circumstances. There is a way, but you will need help in finding it.

Second, understand that there is a difference between being generous and indulging brothers and sisters who are financially irresponsible. I never lend money to anyone, and I do not think that you should either. I am convinced that there are people who have fallen away over money they borrowed from their brothers in Christ and were unable to pay it back. The only instances in which I "loan" money is when I am willing to give it without expecting repayment. If I think the person is irresponsible, I neither give nor lend.

Step Two:
Be Open About Your Finances

Deciding to be generous is only the first step on the road to the kind of financial independence that I believe God wants for you. Where do you go from there? You need to confront your financial fears by being open about your finances. This is an area in which far too many do not ask for discipling.

To begin with, most of us do not have sufficient financial knowledge to even ask the right questions. Second, many of us are hiding our own financial sin, so we do not want to bring up the subject. However, in every congregation and in every ministry within congregations, there are people who are good with handling money, and you need to seek them out and get their help. (Those of you who are good financial managers will find counseling others an excellent way to serve your brothers and sisters).

Step Three:
Establish Financial Goals

The next step is to establish long-range financial goals and write them down. Think in terms of these questions: What would be your ideal lifestyle? What do you consider financial independence? What net worth will allow you to achieve these goals? Pray about these answers. A dangerous byproduct of not writing these goals down is that the net worth which would provide for your definition of financial independence and happiness keeps increasing until you are caught in an "ever-increasing" trap. We must have a predetermined cutoff point. I call it your "I Quit Point": the point at which you quit working to support yourself and work instead to make money to help others. All the while, as you work toward your goal, you must honor God with the firstfruits.

Now, some of you are probably thinking that this is all a bit unrealistic. You are thinking, "Wait a minute! I earn $30,000 a year, and it costs me $33,000 a year to cover my expenses. Every time I get a 10 percent pay increase, my expenses seem to go up by 15 percent." If you are thinking this way, what you have done is basically decided that you are never going to get anything. With this kind of attitude, you never will.

Regardless of your current financial status, you can begin to work toward the goal of financial independence. The answer is simple: Do it a little at a time. Amassing wealth is not just for professionals, stockbrokers or people on Wall Street. My mother, who had a third-grade education and never once earned more than minimum wage in her entire working life, died three years ago and left my brother and me hundreds of thousands of dollars of fully paid-up rental property in Miami. How did she do it? A little bit at a time.

If you cannot increase your income at this time, you must decrease your outgo. A preacher once said, "If your outgo exceeds your income, your upkeep is your downfall." This is the truth! Stop saying that decreasing your expenses is impossible. I know people who are making half a million dollars a year who are saying the same thing. Their problem is the same as yours: spending more than they take in.

In order to break this habit, you need to make three decisions: (1) I will give to God first; (2) I will save for the future; and (3) I will live on what is left. If you do not make these decisions, you will always spend everything you make.

Many of you will give to God, because you feel too guilty if you don't, but you will never save anything. You are in the habit of never having enough money and, like any other bad habit, it needs to be broken. Some of you have spent years carrying a $1,000 to $2,000 balance on a credit card, and now you are just used to it. You're just assuming that this is the kind of shape your finances are always going to be in. Others of you have never saved more than $5,000 but now you feel pretty good about the fact that you have a little put away, so you spend the remainder of your personal income without saving any more.

You need to decide that you will always save, that you will become a saver. Train yourself to be a saver. If you get into the habit, you will always set money aside, and it will start to grow. It will become second nature to you. Look at your budget, and choose a number of areas in which you can save money. Look at where your money is going. Do you eat out once a week? Don't–

it's expensive. Do you go out to the movies? Don't—it doesn't matter if all the other brothers and sisters are doing it and you feel left out. Wait until the movie comes out on video to see it. Don't tell yourself that you have to live a certain way—you don't. Thinking this way will only get you into trouble.

I moved to Miami in 1980. I was a lawyer and a CPA, straight out of school. I was making decent money, and my wife was making decent money. But we ran a little short, and I had to go to my mom to borrow money to buy some furniture. She said to me, "What are you doing with your money? I know families that don't speak English, have three kids, just got off the boat from Cuba and are managing to pay their bills and support their families. You are a lawyer and a CPA, and you don't have enough money to pay your bills! Why don't you plan on living on half of what you're making, and put the rest in the bank?"

It was such a simple concept: Think like an immigrant. My father and mother were divorced in 1975, and he later married a woman from the old Soviet Union. Her family was very well educated and had taught at universities in Russia. Despite their background, she and her family had no shame about what they did to earn money here in America. No job was "beneath" them. They painted houses for a living; they lived three families to a house to save money; and they were not embarrassed. They thought and lived as immigrants.

After our first year in Miami, my wife and I left our fancy apartment in a high-rent district and moved into the inner city into one of the apartments that my mother owned there. It was shabby but clean, and our rent was cut in half. We were not secretive about what we were doing; we invited people over all the time. Some would think nothing of where we lived. Others would react rather negatively and say that they thought we would have a nicer place. I would reply, "No, we're trying to save money."

It was really good for us! We got out of that mentality where we felt we needed a lifestyle that was commensurate with our educational status. We had a change of attitude. After all, a disciple's identity does not consist in what particular rung of the socioeconomic ladder he or she is on. Jesus himself said, "A man's life does not consist in the abundance of his possessions" (Luke 12:15).

Before you can begin to save, however, you need to get out of debt. First, get out of consumer debt, and firmly decide that you will never get into it again. Never, ever buy anything for which you do not have the money in hand. If there is something you really need, wait until you have the money to buy it. If you want a new stereo system that costs $1,500, save up that money first. Believe me, after you have put in the effort to save that amount, the stereo will probably not look nearly as attractive! When you just put that amount onto a credit card and ignore the consequences, then there is no real incentive to be prudent.

Once you have paid off your consumer debt, I think the next thing you should get rid of is your car loan. If you have $10,000 in the bank and a $15,000 car loan, I think you should take the $10,000 and pay down the car loan. Pay your normal monthly payment, even though your monthly payments will now be reduced. This way, you will pay off the loan quicker and have done with it. The amount you used to pay toward your car loan can now go into savings.

Next, if the only thing you have left is a home mortgage, I recommend that you work on paying that off at an accelerated rate, while continuing to save money. This is my philosophy, and not everyone agrees with it. It worked for me. I did not start saving money until about four or five years ago. Because I had already cleared my debt and had no monthly payments, I was able to put away a large sum of money in a relatively short period of time, so that I now only work part-time. During tax season, I make enough money to last the whole year, and the rest of the time I work part-time. Years ago, one of my goals was to be able to work part-time by the time I turned 45. I am now 44, so I made it with a year to spare!

> In the house of the wise there are stores of choice food and oil,
> but a foolish man devours all he has. (Proverbs 21:20)

Do not devour all you have; build your storehouse, always remembering to be generous and to share what you have. Don't become the rich fool of Luke 12. Jesus doesn't admonish him for building his storehouse but for doing so "without being rich toward God." Let your ambition be to free yourself up to do the things you really want to do: spend more time with your family, be more available for the work of the ministry, do more for HOPE *worldwide*, be a self-supported ministry leader—whatever! But beware of financial entanglements, dubious multilevel marketing enterprises and other time-consuming schemes. There is no way to get rich quick. There is, however, a sure way to do it slowly.

> Do not be overawed when a man grows rich,
> when the splendor of his house increases;
> for he will take nothing with him when he dies,
> his splendor will not descend with him. (Psalm 49:16-17)

Do not be impressed at the lifestyles of the rich. In many cases their lifestyle is a front for massive debt, and in others it has cost them dearly and will cost them even more in the future. Build the kind of wealth that will last. Build your storehouse slowly, surely, a little at a time. Provide a safety net for your children, and teach them to do likewise.

Finally, when you really begin to attain the kind of lifestyle that you want, do not feel insecure about it. Use your wealth for the kingdom of God. My wife and I became disciples when we were in college, and Kip McKean was one of our classmates at the time. Kip was a top student, and he challenged us to do our very best also. Most of us graduated with honors, and we were very fruitful also. Do you know who we converted? The top students! From this ministry came many of those who are still leaders in the kingdom today. If we had been a bunch of 'C' students, we would not have attracted the top students with the force that we were able to. Being as successful as we can be is not unspiritual, as long as we guard our hearts and heed the advice and wisdom of the Scriptures. Do not settle for second best! Take hold of the life that God wants you to have: life to the full in every way.

Basic Financial Management

BY MADALINE EVANS

In this chapter I want you to learn how to create a budget, how to spend your money, when to use cash, when to use checks and last but not least, how to get rid of debt. I have some incredible stories to share with you about people who were deeply in debt, then sat down just like I hope you will do today, worked through their finances and came up with a plan to get out and stay out of debt. Many of these people are still thanking me today.

When we do not handle our finances well, it is sinful. Like any other sin, it weighs on us. But there is hope. I want to encourage you to get fully involved in this process. Do not be afraid of the numbers; do not be ashamed; be totally honest. I promise you, if you fully commit to getting on top of your finances, you will feel light and uplifted simply because you have a plan in place. Even if you subsequently mess up, you will be equipped to start over.

The worksheet I will be using is for single people, but if you are married, it is easy enough to adjust it for your needs. There is a blank Budget Worksheet on the following page. (For a much more detailed worksheet see Appendix 2 on page 115.) I will be taking you through a sample budget for a woman whose name is Betsy Broke. Betsy has quite a bit of debt, and she wants to get out of it. Her current financial situation has been outlined in her

Budget Worksheet

1. Total weekly or biweekly take-home pay
   (husband and wife) $_____

2. Total actually spent each month on:

   Contribution |
   Rent/Mortgage |
   Food |
   Gas/Electric/Water |
   Transportation |
   Phone |
   Clothing |
   Cable |
   Haircuts/Hair Care |
   School Activities/Child Care |
   Laundry |
   Entertainment/Dates |
   Miscellaneous |

3. List every outstanding loan you have (credit cards, banks, schools, auto loans, etc.), and every person you owe (doctors, friends, relatives, etc.).

Name	Balance	Monthly Payment	Months Overdue	Interest Rate
1.				
2.				
3.				
4.				
5.				
6.				
7.				
8.				
9.				
10.				
11.				
12.				
13.				
14.				
15.				

Betsy's Budget Worksheet

1. Total weekly or (biweekly) take-home pay
   (husband and wife) $ 700

2. Total actually spent each month on:

   Contribution   170
   Rent/Mortgage – first of the month   400
   Food   525
   Gas/Electric/Water   50
   Transportation   90
   Phone   80
   Clothing ⎤   225
   Cable   ⎥   60
   Haircuts/Hair Care Other   250
   School Activities/Child Care   0
   Laundry ⎥   65
   Entertainment/Dates ⎦   200
   Miscellaneous   100

3. List every outstanding loan you have (credit cards, banks, schools, auto loans, etc.), and every person you owe (doctors, friends, relatives, etc.).

Name	Outstanding Balance	Monthly Payment	Months Overdue	Interest Rate
1. IRS	2000	110	2	15%
2. Sears	800	30	3	14.7
3. Discover	1000	35	1	19.8
4. Citibank	1500	75	4	19.8
5. Macy's	575	45	2	21.6
6. J.C. Penny	350	50	1	21.6
7. Limited	200	35	2	21.6
8.				
9.				
10.				
11.				
12.				
13.				
14.				
15.				

TOTAL MONTHLY PAYMENTS: $380

budget worksheet on the previous page. As we go through Betsy's finances step by step to see how she is doing, substitute your own numbers to come up with a detailed picture of your finances.

Betsy Broke's Budget

Betsy Broke, as you can see from a quick glance at her budget worksheet, is not doing well financially. In fact she is usually unhappy, especially when she is thinking about her finances. It shows in the way she looks, the way she talks, the way she walks. She is feeling heavy. Sadly, many of us can relate. The first thing Betsy needs to do is to figure out exactly where her main financial problems are.

Like most people, Betsy gets paid every two weeks, so we will work with that standard. At the top of Column A on Betsy's Worksheet—First Draft on page 47, I put in the date of Betsy's next pay period, which is May 14. At the top of Column B, I put in the date of the pay period after that, which is two weeks after the date in Column A, or May 28. On your own Six-Week Worksheet (page 48), fill in what your pay will be for the next six pay periods.

The first thing we need to identify is Betsy's living expenses. Betsy, like the rest of us, cannot deal with debt until she has covered these. When we have identified how much of her paycheck is accounted for by living expenses, we can see how much, if anything, she has left available for debt reduction, based on her current spending habits.

Betsy's current gross pay is $850 every two weeks. This is what she earns before taxes are taken out. Her net pay (what is left over after taxes) is $700 every two weeks. This is the amount that is deposited into her account. Now, out of that $700, the first thing she wants to do is to give back to God (Malachi 3:10, Exodus 23:19a). This must be a priority. The feelings of guilt

Betsy's Six-Week Worksheet
First Draft

	5/14	5/28	6/11	6/25	7/9	7/23
1 LIVING EXPENSES:						
2 Contribution	85	85	85	85	85	85
3 Rent	400	400	200	200	200	200
4 Utilities	25	25	25	25	25	25
5 Telephone	185	25	25	25	25	25
6 Transportation	60	60	60	60	60	60
7 Food	263	263	263	263	263	263
8 Other	400	400	400	400	400	400
9 Miscellaneous	100	100	100	100	100	100
10 subtotal	1518	1358	1158	1158	1158	1158
11						
12 AVAILABLE FOR DEBT	<818>	<658>	<458>	<458>	<458>	<458>
13 (row 23 - row 10)						
14 DEBT:						
15 IRS						
16 Sears						
17 Discover						
18 Citibank						
19 Macy's						
20 J.C. Penney						
21 Limited						
22						
23 NET PAY:	700	700	700	700	700	700
24						
25						
26						
27						
28						

Six-Week Worksheet

	(DATE)					
1 LIVING EXPENSES:						
2 Contribution						
3 Rent						
4 Utitities						
5 Telephone						
6 Transportation						
7 Food						
8 Other						
9 Miscellaneous						
10 subtotal						
11						
12 AVAILABLE FOR DEBT:						
13 (row 26 - row 10)						
14 DEBT:						
15						
16						
17						
18						
19						
20						
21						
22						
23						
24						
25						
26 NET PAY:						
27						
28						

that people have when they consistently fail to give the contribution they have pledged are easy for Satan to capitalize on—it is easy to see why people are tempted to fall away because of finances. If Betsy's gross pay every two weeks is $850, and she is committed to tithing, then her weekly contribution is $42.50 (10 percent of $850 divided by two). But remember, since we're working with a budget based on a two-week model, the number Betsy needs to put in the first column is $85, or two weeks of contribution. So substitute what the equivalent figure is for you, and plug that into your worksheet for the next six pay periods.

The next thing we need to put in the worksheet is rent. We cannot plan to live on someone else's money. It is not acceptable to just tell your roommate(s), "I can't pay the rent this month." Betsy's current rent is $400 dollars per month, due on the first of every month. However, true to form, she is late, so she will have to use her May 14 paycheck to pay all of her rent. When she gets paid on May 28, she is going to pay her rent *again*, since it is due on June 1. From that time on, starting on June 11th, she only needs to set aside $200 out of every pay period. You can see the difference in her budget already, just by breaking down her monthly rent expense in a disciplined manner.

Next, we need to take care of utilities: electricity, gas and water. For those who live in apartments, utilities are fairly inexpensive. Betsy's are about $50 per month, and are due by the end of the month. She is going to pay on time, but she still needs to divide up the expense. She will budget $25 from each pay period. That way, when the utility bill comes, she will not be afraid to open up the envelope because she knows she has the money.

The next item is the telephone bill. This is one of the major areas in which people have a tendency to be shortsighted. I have known single people with phone bills of $250 per month! If you are in debt, it cannot be an option for you to use the phone like that. Personally, I refuse to invest in this kind of expense. My challenge to you, especially if you are in debt, is to decide that you will not go over $50 per month for your phone bill. If you have family far away, write. The art of writing has disappeared; bring it back. It only costs 33 cents. If there are certain situations in which you need to call, do it at a time when rates are low and keep yourself to a predetermined time limit. Do whatever you must to keep your monthly phone bill to $50 or less. Once you are out of debt, you can increase that limit if you wish.

Let's go back to Betsy. Her current telephone bill is $185, due now. In fact, some of the previous month's bill is included in there also, along with some late charges. But she is convicted and determined to change. She is going to limit herself to $50 per month after she clears the $185 phone bill with the May 14 paycheck. So we will set aside $25 per pay period for the rest of the worksheet.

Now, concerning your own finances: If you have a large phone bill that goes back several months, don't put it in the "Phone" column. It needs to go down at the bottom of the worksheet, in the debt section. This is an accumulated debt, and we need to have a different plan to deal with that, which we will get to later.

The next thing in Betsy's budget is transportation. She uses the subway to get around, which costs her $120 a month, so she needs to budget $60 per pay period. She has already bought her tokens for the month; now she is just saving for her tokens next month. So we've entered $60 per pay period in her budget worksheet. If you are fortunate enough to have a car, your monthly gasoline, maintenance, repair and auto insurance expenses should be entered in the transportation column of the "living" budget section. Don't enter car loan payments here; they need to go down at the bottom of the worksheet in the accumulated debt column. Enter your monthly payment in each column.

The next living expense is food. Betsy loves to eat and she also has people over and cooks for them quite frequently. As a matter of fact, her food expenses are $525 a month! That's $262.50 per pay period which we will round up to $263 for the worksheet.

Concerning the remaining regular living expenses, in the column marked "Other," we have estimated an amount for items such as clothing, personal care items, unreimbursed medical expenses, laundry and haircuts. You do need to budget something for these items because you need to take care of yourself and look good, even when you are on a strict budget. You need to look good as you share your faith, so keep those items in your budget, although they should be done as inexpensively as possible. If you are married, you may have childcare expenses. (See a more detailed budget form in the back of this book that may be useful to those with more complicated situations).

The next category is entertainment, which is usually a large one for disciples. Betsy has several cable stations, loves to go to the movies and buys lots of new CDs. In fact, when you add up all of these living expenses, Betsy spends $400 every two weeks!

"Miscellaneous" is anything else that we have not covered, either items that you have not thought of, or that you did not foresee. It could be bank charges, ATM fees, church ministry activities that someone forgot to tell you about, birthday or wedding gifts—anything unexpected. For Betsy, "Miscellaneous" added up to about $100 every two weeks.

Something Has to Give!

When we add everything up, Betsy's total living expenses for the current pay period are $1518. However, her income is only $700! She is already spending twice what she earns, and we have not even covered her debt yet. This is called "living beyond your means." How do your figures compare? Don't get discouraged! Things will get better, I promise. The changes Betsy had to make are shown on Betsy's Worksheet–Revised, found on page 53. Work along with me, and tackle your budget in the same manner.

What can Betsy do? Should she cut back on her contribution? No, because she does not want to rob God; she wants him to bless her efforts. Should she not pay her rent? This is not an option. Where can she begin to cut back? The most obvious item is food. In doing budgets with people over the years, I have found that for a single person, a weekly food bill that is tight, but reasonable, is $25 to $35. You will definitely need to live on staple items, but your goal is to get out of debt. This will not last forever; now is the time to get tough. Be creative and become a coupon clipper.

A sister in the New York church became an expert coupon clipper when she was on welfare for several months following a serious operation that required an extended recovery time. Once she purchased $28 worth of groceries for $15 by using coupons, and then mailed in rebates for $20. In other words the store not only gave her $28 worth of groceries free of charge, they also paid her $5 for the privilege! With this kind of creativity, $25 a week for food is not an unreasonable amount for someone on a tight budget. This is the amount that Betsy will enter for her food budget: $50 for each pay period.

Another big drain in Betsy's budget is "Other." This is currently costing her $400 every two weeks. My suggestion about these expenses is that you can only have what you can afford. If you need to go to a less expensive hair salon and so forth, so be it. For example, teaching schools will cut your hair for free. If you live in a big city, there is plenty of free entertainment, especially in the summer months. Be creative. Necessity is the mother of invention. Betsy, in her current situation, should not plan on

Betsy's Six-Week Worksheet

Revised

	5/14	5/28	6/11	6/25	7/9	7/23
1 LIVING EXPENSES:						
2 Contribution	85	85	85	85	85	85
3 Rent	400	400	200	200	200	200
4 Utilities	25	25	25	25	25	25
5 Telephone	185	25	25	25	25	25
6 Transportation	60	60	60	60	60	60
7 Food	25	25	50	50	50	50
8 Other	50	50	50	50	50	50
9 Miscellaneous	50	30	50	50	50	50
10 subtotal	880	700	545	545	545	545
11						
12 AVAILABLE FOR DEBT:	20	0	155	155	155	155
13 (row 23-row10)						
14 DEBT:						
15 IRS			55	55	55	55
16 Sears			25	–	25	–
17 Discover			–	25	–	25
18 Citibank			25	–	25	–
19 Macy's			–	25	–	25
20 J.C. Penney			25	–	25	–
21 Limited	20		25	50	25	50
22						
23 NET PAY:	900*	700	700	700	700	700
24						
25						
26						
27						
28						

*Includes $200 left in her checking account.

spending more than $25 a week for "Other," whatever cuts she needs to make. Let's put that figure into her revised worksheet. In order to get out of debt, entertainment must be kept to $25 per month. No matter what, you should not go beyond a total of $100 a month for "Other."

What about the "Miscellaneous" category? The same principle applies: Decide that you must cut way back. Do only what you can afford. Be wise; get serious with your finances. It will not always be like this, but if you have a large amount of debt, you have got to do this. I suggested to Betsy that for "Miscellaneous," she should allow no more than $25 per week. Let's put that in her revised worksheet.

Now, Betsy's total expenses for the first pay period are still quite large because of the expensive phone bill and the entire month's rent, which are all due by the end of the month. Remember, the amount in the first column cannot go beyond $700 (which is Betsy's net pay). She cannot continue to live beyond her means, and charging further debt to her credit cards is not an option. What can she do? One of the big problems is that overdue phone bill. She needs to call the phone company and ask them to work out a payment plan, which they are usually willing to do. She can also decide to spend even less on food for those periods. She can wash her clothes out by hand for the next two weeks. This may sound drastic, but right now drastic measures are called for.

Betsy also has a couple of hundred dollars in her checking account, which can count toward the amount of money she has available for this pay period. If you are in a similar situation, be sure to include the money you have in your checking account (less outstanding checks) in your current period as well. When Betsy does this, her total available for the May 14 pay period is $900 ($700 net plus $200 in checking).

As soon as she gets of top of things, the picture becomes much rosier. Look at the June 11 pay period, just two pay periods away. Her expenses are down to $545 already! She brings home $700. That means that every two weeks, she already has $155 available for debt servicing. I went through this example to show you what the anatomy of a typical bad budget is. In every budget, there are some items you cannot change, but many that you can. Find the items in your budget that can go, and cut them out.

Betsy Broke's Debt

Now let's talk about Betsy's debt. She owes the IRS, Sears, Discover, Citibank, Macy's, J.C. Penney and the Limited (see Betsy's Budget Worksheet on page 44). Her basic monthly payments total $380, which she does not have at this time. In regard to your debt, add up your current minimum payments. When Betsy did this, she knew it was time for financial advice because even after she cut back on everything and made all the adjustments possible, she still did not have enough to pay all her creditors each month.

So, what can Betsy do about her debt? Well, the first thing she needs to do is cut up every credit card she has—every one! Then she should close out the accounts so she is not tempted again when the replacement cards come in the mail. Basically, I think everyone should have only one credit card. Preferably, this should be an American Express card because you are required to pay your full balance every month. If you cannot get an American Express, then get one department store card (like Macy's or J.C. Penney), and use it for emergencies only. Department stores carry just about everything, so generally they will meet your needs if you have an emergency. Another thing Betsy can do is get a part-time job and earmark that money specifically for debt payments.

The key to tackling debt is this: Figure out how much you have available for debt servicing each month; then decide how much you can pay each creditor, regardless of what they want the monthly payment to be. Pay them the same amount each month without fail. Structure the money you have available for debt so that you can pay a little more each month to the smallest outstanding balance. Number the debts by balances, smallest to largest, and work on repaying them in that order. This way, you will give yourself some encouragement (most people need it when they see the seriousness of their situation!).

For instance, Betsy's smallest debt is to the Limited, which is a clothing store. She should pay this one off as soon as possible. Use any excess cash (and I mean *any!*) to double up on the payments to the smallest outstanding balance. Once your smallest debt is paid off, use the money that has been freed up to pay the next smallest outstanding balance. Keep repeating this until all the money available for debt is being used up—even if you only have one or two outstanding balances left.

Betsy also has some debts that she needs to pay right away simply because of the nature of the debtor. Let's look at the lower half of Betsy's Worksheet–Revised, to see the plan for retiring her debt. For instance she owes the IRS $110 per month. She has not paid the IRS yet this month, so she needs to call them. She should apologize for her delinquency, let them know she is putting herself on a strict budget and tell them that her first payment of $110 will be mailed out on June 25. She needs to promise that she will stick to this arrangement until the debt is paid. The IRS may not be happy with this, but they will take her check nonetheless. In June I would suggest that Betsy divide up the IRS payment, budgeting $55 dollars per pay period for it.

Citibank wants $75 per month which Betsy does not have this month. She needs to call them to let them know she will only be able to pay $25 per month and that she will increase this amount when she can. She is four months behind with her payments to Citibank anyway, so the call will not be a big surprise to them. She should do the same with Macy's, J.C. Penney, Sears and Discover. Once she gets out of the woods over the next couple of pay periods, she can start to pay each creditor more each month. As the debts clear, her feelings of encouragement and determination will grow.

As you can see, she will be able to pay the Limited every paycheck. For the June 25 and July 23 pay periods, she can pay them $50 each time. By the end of July, she will have paid Limited $170. The outstanding balance of $30 (plus interest) will be paid off in August. She can now take the money she was paying to Limited and give it to J.C. Penney, the next smallest balance. This means that payments to J.C. Penney in August will be $25 on August 6, $40 on August 20, $50 on September 3, and $50 on September 17. By the end of September, she will have paid J.C. Penney a total of $215 from an original outstanding balance of $350. By the end of December, Betsy will have paid off Limited, J.C. Penney and most of Macy's—all in a little more than six months.

This process will accelerate significantly if Betsy gets a part-time job. I strongly suggested to her that she do this. If she gets a job for 15-20 hours a week (which should earn her about $400 a month), she can pay off the Limited with her first or second paycheck! Imagine how good that will feel. The next part-time paychecks can pay off J.C. Penney. When her debts have been paid, Betsy can quit her part-time job, as long as she has learned to live within the income from her full-time job.*

*Editor's note: *There are some very reputable, national, nonprofit organizations that specialize in helping people get out of credit card debt. They will often be able to negotiate lower interest rates while you are paying off the debt. Their monthly fees are typically as low as $20. Check the yellow pages or the World Wide Web, or ask financial advisers in your congregation for their names.*

A tip that many people have found useful in controlling their spending is to only carry cash for what you need on any given day. I hardly ever carry cash with me; I may carry $5 or $10 at the most. Cash goes too fast. If you have it with you, you are much more likely to spend it. If, like Betsy, you have a budget allowing you only $25 to cover all miscellaneous expenses for a full two weeks, you need to be extra careful with your cash. Another tip is to use checks for everything you can.

For expenses that you must have cash for, start an envelope system: Every week, go to the ATM and withdraw the amount of cash you need for that week's expenses only. For Betsy, this is $30 for transportation, and $25 each for food, miscellaneous and other, totaling $105 per week—not a penny more. When you get back home, take out some plain white envelopes, and put the allotted cash for each expense in separate envelopes. Have one envelope marked "Food," another marked "Transportation," and so on. This is how you budget for the week. If you want to get some food and the "Food" envelope is empty, what do you do? Eat what you already have. It will only be empty for a few days at most, because you have the money in the bank for the next week's needs. The envelope method is great for teaching discipline, if you will let it. Do not be tempted to go into one of the other envelopes if you run out of money: This is a bad habit! Or sometimes the opposite happens: At the end of a particular week you have money left over in one or more envelopes, and you think, "Great! I have some extra money to spend." No! Keep the money there. By doing this, you are prepared if for some reason you have unexpected "Other" or "Miscellaneous" expenses the following week.

There Is a Lot of Hope

To close out, let me give you some stories to encourage you. I have done budgets with many, many people. Those who really commit themselves to their new budget always come back with some great victories to tell me about. I really believe that when we are serious about repenting, God blesses us in a tremendous way. The last thing I tell people when we are finished with their budget is to pray. Let God know how serious you are about repenting. I tell them that they are going to get money from places they had never imagined. The only thing I ask them to do is to call me back and tell me about the victories! (Galatians 6:6).

One woman came to me $35,000 in debt, and she was out of debt in two years. She has just bought a car and has an apartment of her own, with her name on the lease. She recently told me that she has never felt so free in her life. Another woman, a single mom on welfare, went through her finances with me, and she could not see how she was ever going to get out of debt. Again, I told her to pray and stick faithfully to her new budget. Two days later, she called me. Her children's father, whom she had not seen in fifteen years, walked into her house and gave her a huge sum of money.

Another couple in the ministry in New York were slated to go on a mission team, but they could not go because they had such a huge amount of debt, approximately $30,000. They were very serious about getting out of debt: They tore up all their cards, didn't use the ATM, and went on a strict budget. A few months later, they called to tell me that their landlord wanted to buy them out of their apartment. They were in a rent-controlled apartment, and the landlord knew it would be better for him if he bought them out of their lease. He offered them $30,000!

If you have any questions at all about your finances as you get on your new plan, seek advice. It is out there in abundance if you will look for it, and because you are part of God's kingdom, it probably will not cost you a penny. You need to teach yourself to handle and spend money correctly, which you have not so far been able to do if you are in serious debt. Get radical, and get ready for God to do more than you could ever ask for or imagine!

Investment Basics

BY DANIEL H. BATHON, JR. & ROBERT GAUNTT

Putting God First

BY DANIEL H. BATHON, JR.

In 1986 my income, as a member of a famous Wall Street firm, was a fairly hefty $500,000. Contrary to some other people you will read about in this book, however, my income steadily decreased from there. I moved to Paris that year as a self-supported member of a mission team, and my income for the next couple of years was a "mere" $300,000. Then I started my own company in Paris, and my income promptly went down to around $175,000. Since then I have been working for the kingdom, and my income has further decreased.

But there are many different ways to be blessed by God. In 1986 Michael Milken, a man I used to work for and whom I still consider a friend, made $285 million. The following year he made $550 million. During the period when my income was plummeting, his was soaring. However, some of you have read about Michael's subsequent criminal conviction and prison time, and now his battle with cancer. I know I would not swap places with him or any other Wall Street baron for anything.

We want to pass on to you in this chapter some valuable information and help you to learn to be a better investor, but your overriding desire must be to put God first. Your financial life should enhance your spiritual life, not damage it. Before you can learn to be a solid investor, you must understand that money has a sinful pull on people, both on those who have it and those who desire it. In Matthew 13:22, Jesus is explaining the Parable of the Sower. He says,

> *The one who received the seed that fell among the thorns is the man who hears the word, but the worries of this life and the deceitfulness of wealth choke it, making it unfruitful.*

Wealth can be deceitful, so we must guard our hearts. I would sooner make it to heaven dirt poor than be as rich as Bill Gates and not make it.

I did not always think this way. Before I became a disciple, my goal in life was to make a lot of money. My goals were simple: I wanted to be earning $100,000 per year by the time I was 30 and have a net worth of a million dollars. I achieved both of these goals. Since then, however, I have learned firsthand that the size of your bankbook has no bearing whatsoever upon your level of happiness. As Paul says in 1 Timothy 6:6-9:

> *But godliness with contentment is great gain. For we brought nothing into the world, and we can take nothing out of it. But if we have food and clothing, we will be content with that. People who want to get rich fall into temptation and a trap and into many foolish and harmful desires that plunge men into ruin and destruction.*

In 1987 when I was in Paris, the New York stock market crashed, and I lost $60,000 in a single day. At the time, that represented no more than a couple months' income, so in relative terms it was not a very large sum of money. But that day I went home completely heartsick because I was furious with myself for not getting out of the market sooner. I realized that even though I was a disciple, money still owned me. It was still lodged too deeply in my heart. Black Monday, as that day came to be known, was a great lesson for me. I was a disciple, but I was not out of the spiritual risk zone when it came to money— not by a long shot.

A few years later I invested $200,000 in a business that was owned by a brother. For a while the stock did extremely well. At one time the company was valued at $6 million, and I owned 50 percent of it. Six months later it went bankrupt, and I started having suspicious and bitter thoughts: *What had the brother done with my money? How could this happen? What did he do wrong?* My trust in this brother plummeted, until I thought about Luke 6:34-35, which says:

> *"And if you lend to those from whom you expect repayment, what credit is that to you? Even 'sinners' lend to 'sinners,' expecting to be repaid in full. But love your enemies, do good to them, and lend to them without expecting to get anything back. Then your reward will be great, and you will be sons of the Most High, because he is kind to the ungrateful and wicked."*

I vividly remember reading this scripture and being cut to the heart about my sinful feelings about my brother. I had to ask myself, did the money mean that much to me that I would harbor this anger in my heart and let it destroy my relationship with my brother? My answer was sadly yes. I got down on the floor and cried out to God to forgive me for my greedy feelings. I prayed earnestly for God to move my heart to compassion, not bitterness.

I had to do two things in that situation. First, I had to forgive my brother. I had to get to the point where I could fully accept in my heart that it was just money. I wish I had been a

better steward with it, but bottom line that is all it was. It was
not worth my being divisive with my brother. Second, I had to
forgive the debt. I drove several hours and went to the brother
and told him that he owed me nothing. He had to know that I
forgave him and expected nothing from him. That was a turn-
ing point in our relationship; we drew closer and we are still
great friends today as a result.

The key element of this story is that I was not "discipled" to
do this; no one challenged me to forgive; no, it was simply the
word of God applied to my sinner's heart that compelled me to
ask for God's forgiveness and allowed me to forgive in return.
No amount of money can buy that! These financial crises taught
me some priceless lessons. Most of all, I have learned—the hard
way—that my possessions, like your possessions, belong to God.
He has given them to us, and he can take them away whenever
he chooses. I believe he will, if they begin to threaten our relationship with him. We are simply baby-sitting his possessions
until he chooses to use them for his purposes. We can enjoy
them, we need to share them, but we need to remember to whom
they ultimately belong:

> *"From everyone who has been given much, much will be de-*
> *manded; and from the one who has been entrusted with much,*
> *much more will be asked." (Luke 12:48b)*

Real Worth

BY ROBERT GAUNTT

My background is somewhat similar to Dan's, in that my
financial goal was to become very wealthy at a young age. I
grew up in a family that had the appearance of being rich, but
was in actuality very poor. As a result, I developed a real fear of

financial insecurity and was determined from a fairly young age that my own kids would never have to go through those kinds of experiences. Therefore, my whole life was oriented toward making money.

When I graduated from business school, I got a job at one of the most prestigious firms on Wall Street. It took thirty interviews, but they hired me. I was set. All my goals were checked off. I had the great job, great salary, great wife. But I was very unhappy. This was a very scary situation for me, because I had to begin to accept that the things I had sought for so long were simply not enough.

Thankfully, I began to study the Bible and became a disciple in New York, which saved my marriage and my life. At that point, I gave up the goal of becoming wealthy and set before myself the goal of being excellent.

Many disciples today are not excellent in what they do. More specifically, they are not excellent in their finances. Jesus was excellent in all he did, and we need to imitate him (Mark 7:37). My purpose when I go to work today is not to make money; my purpose is to be excellent and to win the respect of people. The sin of financial irresponsibility is something that is not talked about enough in the kingdom of God. More people leave the church in the period immediately before our annual missions contributions than at any other time of the year. The fact of the matter is that people struggle with giving to the church when they are trying to feed their kids, put themselves through school and so on. Therefore my goal in helping to write this book is not to make you richer, but to help you avoid these kinds of traps by being excellent in your finances.

The Basics

BY DANIEL H. BATHON, JR. AND ROBERT GAUNTT

There are three very good reasons why we should invest money. First, the Bible speaks about it. Consider this scripture:

Moreover, when God gives any man wealth and possessions, and enables him to enjoy them, to accept his lot and be happy in his work—this is a gift of God. He seldom reflects on the days of his life, because God keeps him occupied with gladness of heart. (Ecclesiastes 5:19-20)

Money is a gift from God, and we need to view it as such. Our net worth is not what it is because of us (when we start thinking that way we're in big trouble), but we have it because God has decided to use us as a vessel in this particular way. Both of us are very conscious of this fact, and we give back to God and to others accordingly. We are very open about how much we make and want to be constantly called to a high standard of generosity.

Another relevant scripture is Matthew 25:14-30, otherwise known as the Parable of the Talents. In this parable a man goes on a journey and gives his three servants five, two and one talent, respectively. The servant who had been given five talents makes five more, the servant with two talents makes two more, but the servant who had been given one talent does nothing with it. Let's look at the conversation between the one-talent man and the master:

"Then the man who had received the one talent came. 'Master,' he said, 'I knew that you are a hard man, harvesting where you have not sown and gathering where you have not scattered seed. So I was afraid and went out and hid your talent in the ground. See, here is what belongs to you.'

"His master replied, 'You wicked, lazy servant! So you knew

that I harvest where I have not sown and gather where I have not scattered seed? Well then, you should have put my money on deposit with the bankers, so that when I returned I would have received it back with interest.

"'Take the talent from him and give it to the one who has the ten talents. For everyone who has will be given more, and he will have an abundance. Whoever does not have, even what he has will be taken from him. And throw that worthless servant outside, into the darkness, where there will be weeping and gnashing of teeth.'" (Matthew 25:24-30)

The amount of money you have is not the issue. The issue is what you do with what you have. Even the servant with two talents got credit from his master for making something with the little he had. You have a responsibility to handle well what is given to you. You are a disciple of Christ, and you need to be excellent in how you handle what God has given you. Another useful passage on this subject is found in 2 Corinthians 9:6:

Remember this: Whoever sows sparingly will also reap sparingly, and whoever sows generously will also reap generously.

This principle is found throughout the Bible: We reap what we sow. If we sow greed, selfishness and materialism, we will reap what is appropriate to that. Likewise, if we are being irresponsible with our money, we will reap destruction from that. Financial insecurity in families causes more tension than virtually anything else. It is a weapon of Satan that we need to do everything in our power to take out of his hands.

A second reason to invest money is to provide for future family security. As we mentioned above, money is the single greatest source of conflict among married couples in the church. Brothers, when we are financially irresponsible, our wives become insecure. You need to think about the future, and start planning for it right away. If you are young and you plan to get married and have children, you need to start thinking about their college education right away. Don't wait until your children are seventeen and then have to tell them you cannot help them with college because you had not planned ahead for it.

The bottom line is that if you struggle financially, you are going to struggle spiritually. The only way out of this trap is to be financially responsible, starting today. Educate yourself about disciplined, responsible investing.

The third and most important reason to invest is because of the impact it can have for the kingdom of God. As we will see a little later on, the amount of money that could be generated by disciples through good financial habits is nothing short of mind-boggling. We have a responsibility to do our best to build God's kingdom for the future. Despite the impressive growth statistics that we have become used to hearing, there is a long, long way to go before the world is won for Christ. We need to have a long-term perspective when it comes to helping the kingdom.

Common Mistaken Beliefs

The three keys to beginning investing are to learn as much as you can about investing, seek lots of advice and proceed with caution. In this book we can merely give you some basic pointers, but hopefully they will be enough to whet your appetite. To begin with, let's take a look at some common mistaken beliefs about investing.

1.) Stocks increase in value forever.

At the time of this writing, this seems especially true. For months now the market, with a few exceptions, has been rapidly increasing. If you are not in the market, you start to feel like you are missing out, and you want some of the action. A commonly made mistake is to buy into the latest hot tip, get burned, lose some money, and decide that investing is just not for us. The truth is that over long periods of time, stocks will provide better returns than cash and bonds.

2.) The stock market is just legalized gambling.

Disciplined investing is *not* gambling. Gambling is when you jump on the latest hot tip without doing your homework and throw away money unnecessarily. Investing in good, solid companies has proven over time to render a better return than either cash or bonds.

3.) The market is going to crash.

If you believe this one, you will wait for an "opportune" time to invest—when the market seems "secure." In reality, timing the market is both impossible and costly. It has been tried over and over again. From time to time whiz kids come up with a magic formula that is supposed to be able to predict market trends. Time and again they have been proven unreliable. The best plan is to invest in reliable companies that perform solidly over the long term.

4.) I can make more money buying cheap stocks.

Cheap stocks are cheap for a reason! "Cheap" is a relative term: Bad companies always look cheap, and great companies always look expensive. We know people who are looking for the next Microsoft, so they bought Novell. However, Novell has been a very poor performer for the last six years, and Microsoft shares have increased 1500 percent in the same period. Avoid chasing the "penny stocks" (stocks costing less than $1.00) in the hope of doubling or tripling your income. They are tempting but remember that they are cheap for a reason.

5.) I don't know enough to get started.

This is understandable. Just don't stop there. The mistake we often make, as a result of ignorance, is that we freeze up, do nothing and keep our money in the bank, where it will earn a measly four to five percent interest per year. There are many ways to learn about investing. There are honest brokers who can help. The Internet is a great source of information, and there are plenty of newspapers, books and magazines available. (We will give you some suggestions before we finish.)

6.) My losers will come back double down, and my winners will go down, so I'll sell and take my profits.

In other words we water the weeds and pick the flowers. We take the good stocks out of our portfolios and throw more money at bad stocks. We do not want to be a loser, and we think that selling a stock that is down means we are losers. Stick with your winners. Get rid of your losers. Not the other way round.

The Power of Disciplined Investing

Historic Returns of Various Asset Classes

Asset Class	1945-95 Annualized Returns	Tax Adjusted Return	Tax/ Inflation Adjusted Return
S&P 500	12.4%	8.3%	4.3%
Small Cap Stocks	14.7%	10.1%	5.8%
Venture Capital	15.7%	11.3%	7.0%
T-Bills	4.7%	2.8%	-1.5%
US Long Treasury Bonds	5.5%	3.2%	-1.1%

Figure 1

In general, investing is for long-term profits—at least ten years. Figure 1 lists a history of returns for various forms of investment over a 50-year period. The S&P 500 represents 500 stocks that together form a good cross-section of major American companies. Small Cap stocks represent smaller, emerging companies. Venture Capital investing entails investing in private rather than in publicly traded companies. Since most Venture Capital investments are in new start-up companies, the risk and therefore the potential returns are greater than buying established, mature companies like Coca-Cola, Boeing or Microsoft. Treasury Bills and Bonds are US Government-backed debt obligations. They pay interest and have fixed maturities. The important lesson from this chart is that, after the returns of these different asset classes are adjusted for the average rate of inflation over the past 50 years, investing in bonds or treasury bills loses money. Therefore the only sure means of growing your net worth over time is with stocks.

Returns of 4 Selected Stocks

Company	Purchase Price(1) (Date)	Current Price (12/31/98)	Total Return	Compounded Annual Return
Wal-Mart	$5.81 (12/31/86)	$81.50	1301%	26%
Dell Comp. Corp	$0.19 (6/30/88)	$73.25	37,372%	75%
Cisco Systems	$0.37 (6/30/90)	$92.81	25,117%	92%
Coca-Cola	$4.72 (12/31/86)	$67.00	1,320%	27%

(1) Adjusted for stock splits over holding period.

Figure 2

Figure 2 shows stock returns for four familiar companies. Note that for most of them the purchase price (i.e., the value of the stock when it was originally purchased) is *prior* to the market crash of 1987. In other words, good, solid stocks will increase their value over time despite market fluctuations. This is not intended as a pitch for these companies; we are not recommending that you should go out and buy these particular stocks. The point is that solid companies do well in the long term. They are not that affected by the daily or weekly ups and downs of the market.

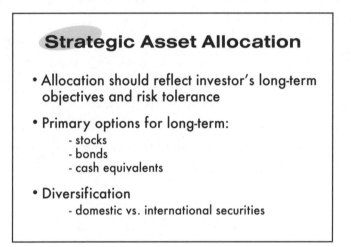

Figure 3

Your stock allocation (the kind of stocks you decide to invest in) should reflect your long term objectives and risk tolerance. What exactly are you planning for? What kind of net worth are you aiming for? You also need to assess your risk tolerance. In general, the greater the risk, the greater the potential for return. Could you live with the possibility that your stocks could lose 25 percent of their worth in a year? If not, then your portfolio needs to be structured accordingly. Would you be happy with a solid 10 percent gain year after year? If so, then you should buy stocks accordingly.

For those who will need all their retirement savings to live out their later years:

- 25 to 50 years of age: 70 to 90% stocks; 10 to 20% bonds; 5% cash
- 50 to 65 years of age: declining balance of stocks to about 50/50 stocks and bonds at 65.
- 65 to 75 years of age: further declining balance of stocks to 25% stocks; 75% bonds.

The challenge of making these kinds of estimates is that you must consider each individual's or couple's situation, such as: What are their annual retirement expenses? Is their house paid for? What is their net worth? For example a couple at age 65 with $2.5 million in liquid investments and who owns their home could comfortably stay with 75 percent stocks all the way up to age 75—and perhaps beyond.

After determining the proper allocation between stocks, bonds and cash, you should then decide on the appropriate allocation within the stock allocation. A good starting point is 65 to 75 percent of your stocks in US companies and 25 to 35 percent international, primarily European and Asian.

Common Financial Profile

- **Joe and Suzy Faithful**

Joint Annual Income	$50,000
Tithe/Sacrifice	$7,000
Cost of Living	$35,000
Misc. Expenses	$3,000
Total Disposable Non-Emergency Funds (DNE)	$5,000

Figure 4

Figure 4 lists a fairly typical financial profile for a married couple in the kingdom. Their joint annual income is $50,000, and when all of their living expenses have been take care of, they have in the neighborhood of $5,000 left over, which we will call DNE, disposable non-emergency funds. This is not money that you are keeping in the bank for an emergency. (Most financial advisers recommend that you should have three months' worth of living expenses in the bank at any given time.) This is money that you have totally freed up for investment purposes by getting your family budget in order.

Investment of Non-Emergency Funds

Disposable Non-Emergency Funds (DNE): $5,000

Assumptions:
- Time Frame: 10 Years
- Initial Investment: $500
- Monthly Installments: $416
- Inflation: 2.5%
- Tithe: 15%

Figure 5

Let's invest the $5,000 (see Figure 5). Let's say your initial investment is $500, and after you allow for inflation and tithing, you make a monthly payment to your investment account of $416, for the next 10 years.

Effects of Compounding Returns
YEAR 10

Investment Plan	Capital Appreciation (Pre-tax)	Kingdom Tithe
Plan A: 100% Cash	$8,200	$1,230
Plan B: 20% Stocks; 80% Bonds and Cash	$14,000	$2,100
Plan C: 100% Stocks	$27,000	$4,050
Plan D: No Savings	$0	$0

Figure 6

Now take a look at Figure 6, which shows what kind of returns you would get with different investment strategies. The Capital Appreciation column lists what your return is *in addition* to the money you have invested. Plan A shows the return from keeping your money in the bank, and as you can see it is very modest indeed. You would have $8,200 after 10 years. Plan B is a very conservative portfolio, mainly bonds and cash with 20 percent stock investments thrown in, and has a fairly healthy return ($14,000 at the end of the 10 years). Plan C is an aggressive portfolio made up entirely of stocks and assumes a modest 10 percent annual return (the market has done more like 17 percent over the past several years). As you can see, the return is very handsome indeed ($27,000 for the 10-year period). Plan D shows what happened when you ate meals out and spent all your money, leaving you with nothing. In the right hand column of this chart, you will see a tithe listed, because the assumption is that you will be tithing on the money that you make in the market, which hopefully you will be.

Church Impact of Tithing Returns
YEAR 10

	Capital Appreciation (Pre-tax)	Kingdom Tithe	NYC # of Disciples	Total Church Impact
Plan A:	$8,200	$1,230	10,000	$12,300,000
Plan B:	$14,000	$2,100	10,000	$21,000,000
Plan C:	$27,000	$4,050	10,000	$40,500,000
Plan D:	$0	$0	10,000	$0

Figure 7

Now let's look at Figure 7, which demonstrates the impact this could have on the finances of a church like, say, the New York City church. The figures are staggering: Even with very conservative investment strategies, the *tithe* of the money earned 10 years from now would be $21 million. With a more aggressive portfolio, the amount would be in excess of $40 million! (This assumes a modest seven percent annual growth rate in the size of the New York congregation, which of course is a bald insult to Steve and Lisa Johnson and all the incredible Big Apple disciples!)

Planning to Invest

Your asset allocation (what combination of stocks, bonds, and cash you put your money in) depends upon three factors that we have briefly discussed: the amount you plan to invest annually, the time frame over which you plan to invest, and your risk tolerance.

The first step is finding out what your DNE is. This is a discipling issue: You need to sit down with someone who is good with finances and budgets and determine a realistic figure that you can set aside every month for investment.

Second, you need to decide on a time frame. Most of you should plan on investing in mutual funds, which are investment vehicles that own various stocks selected by a professional. You do not want to have to spend time every day looking at the computer screen, trying to decide which stocks to buy when there are people whose job is to do that for you. In fact the exuberant stock market over the last four years has lulled many individuals into a false sense of investing acumen. Be careful and be watchful, especially in the area of day trading, as this strategy has wrecked so-called professional traders. Remember that by investing you are putting your money at risk. However, by determining the proper allocation to stocks and by taking a long-term perspective, you will keep your emotions in check and let your portfolio grow.

Third, risk tolerance needs to be determined. Again, what level of risk are you willing to tolerate? Can you stay invested if the stock market were to go down 25 percent, or will you sell to avoid further pain?

Investment Vehicles

COMPANY RETIREMENT PLANS

If you have a 401(k) plan at work and they match any funds you put in, you would be foolish not to take full advantage of it. It is wise to put as much money as you can into these. The company matches it, and it is also tax-advantaged. In other words, the capital gains in these portfolios accrue tax-free. You also cannot touch them without penalty until retirement. Additionally, depending on your age and time until retirement, you should look to maximize the allocation to stocks, as the early withdrawal penalty forces you to stay with a long-term investment horizon.

MUTUAL FUNDS

Mutual funds are what I believe most disciples should be considering. You can call mutual fund companies like Fidelity, Janus and Vanguard and ask them to send you some prospectuses. Look at the style of the fund. Is it small cap? Is it aggressive? Is it fixed income? Look at the investment philosophy. Is it short-term or long-term trading? (You need to know because these are taxed differently.) Look at the track record. Do not put your money into fashionable stocks. Because a stock was featured in *Barrons* that week does not necessarily mean that it is a good stock—someone just happens to be promoting it that week. Stocks like this may increase by five points in a day and then decrease by 15 during the next couple of weeks. A mutual fund's latest track record is not as important as its performance over the last five or 10 years. How did they do in 1991 when we had a tough market? Look at the size of the fund and the companies they own. Are they limited to one sector, i.e. technology, or diversified across many sectors of the economy such as retail, pharmaceuticals, etc. You should focus on investing in mutual funds that take the latter, more diversified approach, as this will give you more protection in a difficult market environment. Always beware of the front end (when you buy) and back end (when you sell) expenses that can be costly. Ask questions.

There are a lot of mutual fund companies that will take a direct deposit from your paycheck every month—this way you are not even tempted to spend the money instead of investing it. This is a fantastic way to save. In fact my wife and I know exactly what it costs for us to live on a monthly basis, and we withdraw all excess funds from our checking account and deposit them into our investment account. This helps us to stay disciplined with our finances and look longer term, as opposed to being tempted to overspend our surplus.

Information Sources

As is hopefully clear to you by now, investing is not something to rush into. Take the time to plan and educate yourself. I would recommend reading magazines like *Money* , *Smart Money or Kiplinger* magazines. There are several books by Peter Lynch that I would also recommend for those interested. The Internet is also a great source for information. Here are some useful Websites:

CBSMarketwatch.com
Fund.com
THEStreet.com
Quicken.com
Morningstar.com
AOL (They have a great finance section)
Investors.com

There are even some sites where you can fill out a questionnaire and get some allocation advice based on the information you give them. The Fidelity mutual fund page is one of those. A word of warning: If you e-trade on the Internet, be careful. On days when trading is very heavy, e-traders sometimes cannot get their orders filled because of congestion and may lose a lot of money while the institutional orders (i.e. orders from brokerage houses etc.) are being filled.

Finally, here are a few words about appreciated stock. If you sell stock options that you received from your company or stock that you received as a gift from your parents, you will pay full capital gains tax on the sale. Since, however, you are giving to the church on a regular basis anyway, it makes infinitely more sense to give the stock directly to the church, rather than selling the stock and giving cash. By law, the church pays no capital gains tax when it sells stock, and you can still take a full deduction for tax purposes. When you do the entire math, it works out that the government is subsidizing your gift to the church to the tune of around 70 percent. It is an incredible savings, and if you are planning to liquidate stock anyway, it is in everyone's best interests to give it directly to the church.

In conclusion, let go and let God. Get out of the way! Stay grateful to be a disciple, stay open about your finances and continue changing your character, and over the years you will be able to save little by little. As Greg Garcia has noted elsewhere in this book, God does want us to have the desires of our hearts, but that is predicated on our staying close to God. No hot stock or investment strategy can ever take the place of that!

Where There's a Will,
There's a Way

BY JOHN BRINGARDNER

In this chapter I want to talk about some basics that will help you plan out your estate. I want to give you God's perspective on the subject. A lot of us in the church have a somewhat warped mindset about this issue, and we do not plan for the future the way that God expects us to. Many disciples think that estate planning, saving money and buying a home are somehow unspiritual, materialistic concerns, but they are not.

The concept of inheritance is introduced early in the Bible. God gives an inheritance to Abraham: He promises him that his children will be as numerous as the stars in the sky and that through his lineage would one day come the Messiah. The Book of Numbers is largely concerned with how God is going to give his people their inheritance, allotting specific areas of land to specific tribes. The Book of Joshua details how the people of Israel go about taking possession of their inheritance.

One of the earliest recorded familial disputes over an inheritance occurs in Judges 11. Jephthah was the son of a prostitute and was driven from his home by his brothers because they did not want him to share in their inheritance. In 1 Kings 21 we read about a man named Naboth who owned a vineyard that was his by inheritance. King Ahab wanted it, but Naboth would not give it up. Ahab consequently schemed with his wife Jezebel to have Naboth put to death.

There are numerous references to inheritances in the New Testament. In the Parable of the Tenants (Matthew 21), the tenants kill the owner of a vineyard's son because they want the vineyard as an inheritance. Matthew 25 contains the Parable of the Sheep and the Goats. The sheep, we are told, receive an inheritance because of the good they had done. In Luke 12 Jesus tells the Parable of the Rich Fool in response to two men who came to him arguing about their inheritance.

Today people in this country and around the world are fighting, scheming and hating one another because someone has not taken proper care of their estate and made provision for what should happen to their inheritance. If you do not plan your estate correctly, you are going to create major problems for people you love. It is that simple.

As we talk here about wills, I want to give one caution. Do not lose sight of the most important inheritance of all:

> *Praise be to the God and Father of our Lord Jesus Christ! In his great mercy he has given us new birth into a living hope through the resurrection of Jesus Christ from the dead, and into an inheritance that can never perish, spoil or fade—kept in heaven for you, who through faith are shielded by God's power until the coming of the salvation that is ready to be revealed in the last time. (1 Peter 1:3-5)*

The greatest inheritance you have is from God—and the greatest inheritance you can give comes from God. While we do want to take care of our families and friends, what you have to offer in Jesus Christ is infinitely more valuable than any material blessing you are able to give.

Having said that, God still wants you to plan. In Proverbs 13:22, the Bible says,

A good man leaves an inheritance for his children's children,
but a sinner's wealth is stored up for the righteous.

Ask yourself this question: Am I a good man or a good woman, by the Bible's standards? Have I left an inheritance for my children's children? Or have I left them empty wishes, broken promises and anger?

God wants us to take care of our families and our finances. Paul, in 1 Timothy 5:8, says that he who does not take care of his immediate family "has denied the faith and is worse than an unbeliever." Our concern for our family must extend beyond the time of our death. In most cases our families will be here after we are gone. Loving your family means providing for them now and planning for what will happen after you are gone.

Not Very 'Will'ing

Not many people have wills. In the US, more than 60 percent of people who should have one do not. I am an attorney who should know better, but even I did not think about doing my own will until about five years ago, when I had two young children and was about to take a long flight overseas. Why is this the case? I suspect there are several main reasons. First, death is not a popular topic. Most of you do not get together with friends and say, "Hey, let's talk about death awhile!" On some level, even as disciples, we are afraid of death, or at least uncomfortable with it. We like to put our head in the sand and pretend that it is not going to happen. But it is—all of us are eventually going to die, and we need to be ready.

Another reason people do not have wills is that they are nervous about attorneys in general and attorney's fees in particular. Many attorneys over-mystify the process of law, which makes it intimidating. Therefore, we are less inclined to work out our legal issues. For the layman, reading the language of legal documents is enough to make the eyes glaze over! As for attorney's fees, many charge astronomically for relatively simple procedures. When I was a young attorney, fresh out of law school, I can remember that our law firm would charge as much as $1,000 for a simple will!

The most prevalent reason people do not have a will is simply that their good intentions do not get converted into action. We plan on doing it, we realize we ought to do it, but we never seem to get around to it. But the time is now! If you have people depending on you, do not wait until it is too late. Remember, where there is a will, there is a way. Where there is no will, there may be unnecessary pain and trouble for those you love.

What Is a Will?

A will is a legal document that becomes effective at your death and details how you want to divide up your property. Everyone who has a child or assets needs one. If you do not have a will, after your death your estate will go through a court procedure called "intestate." This is detrimental for three reasons. First, your estate will be divided up by whim and not according to your wishes. A judge who knows neither you, your family, nor your wishes, will do as he or she sees fit with your money. Your case is probably just one of a hundred files he or she has to read that day. A judge may quite rightly conclude that since you did not take care of your estate while you were living, it must not have been very important to you.

Second, if you do not have a will, the court is going to appoint an executor to administer your estate. Typically, a judge will likely appoint a friend of theirs, as executor of an estate when none has been appointed. In most states the executor gets a percentage of what the estate is worth—as much as 12 percent.

How would you like 12 percent of your estate to go to someone you do not know for simply filing a handful of court papers? Let's see, 12 percent of $100,000...that is a $12,000 bite out of your estate! That is money that should go to your children or grandchildren, but will not if you did not take the time to draft a will.

Third, and most important, if you die without a will as a Christian, there is no guarantee that your children will be raised in a Christian home. If there were no other reason to have a will, this would be enough. You need to make sure that your children are going to have the correct kind of spiritual guidance in the event of your death. My chief concern in drafting a will for my wife and me was for strong, faithful disciples to raise our children.

Can I Draft My Own Will?

It is possible to draft your own will if you have the time and patience to do the groundwork. In all likelihood, however, you will not do it yourself because you have not done it already. If you are determined to do it and feel that you can do the research to make sure it is a legally sound document, go ahead. (Software is available these days to help you with the task.) In most cases, however, it is probably a better idea to have an attorney take care of the details.

Whichever course you choose, some legal requirements must be met. First of all, you must be at least 18 years of age, which probably covers almost all readers of this book. Second, you need to be of "sound mind." Basically, all that means is that you have common sense enough to know that you are dealing with a will and not a birthday card.

The third requirement is that no one has undue influence over the contents of your will, in order to try to have you leave them money. As general counsel for the International Churches of Christ, I have been personally involved with several cases in which people in the church have left substantial amounts of money (in excess of a million dollars) to the church. Some of these have been problematic. We had one case in which a brother who had been in a terrible accident and was paralyzed made the decision to leave all of his money to the church. It was a case of what the Bible describes as "zeal without knowledge." His family, who had been estranged from him, was furious. Had I spoken to the young man in question, I would have dissuaded him from making this kind of decision, because it just invites problems. His family's objections were, I think, quite reasonable. I got involved, and we eventually reached a settlement that satisfied all parties.

Another situation concerned a woman who had cancer and knew she was going to die. She had no immediate family, so she decided to leave everything to the church. After her death a first or second cousin appeared out of nowhere and took the case to court, claiming that the church was a cult and that her cousin had been brainwashed. In this case we did not even know that the sister in question had left her money to the church until after her death. Therefore, as a matter of principle, we felt that we should litigate this matter, especially because we were on sound legal footing. These types of situations will happen, and money has a tendency to bring out the worst in people. Be wise, pray and seek advice about the specifics of your will.

The final requirement is that your will be typewritten. (The only exception to this is under certain circumstances in New Jersey, and even then I would not recommend it.) Also, your will must name an executor, someone you empower to carry out the details of your will after your death. You must then sign and date your will in the presence of two or more witnesses.

How Does the Will Work?

First of all, a will is not effective until your death. Of course at that point, it will be too late to do anything about it, so get it right before you go. All wills go through a legal process known as probate. Probate begins when your executor finds your will and hires an attorney to legally carry out your wishes. Ideally, the attorney should be someone the executor knows and trusts. The attorney files an application with the court and attaches the will to it. The judge then files letters of administration, which are basically permission for the executor to carry out your stated wishes. If you have children under 18, your designated guardians will be empowered to take care of them.

Your executor then collects any outstanding debts, should you have any, and also pays off any and all creditors. When that is done, your money and property are divided up in accordance with your wishes. (Should you die with large debts, you can expect your family to get little or nothing or even to be saddled with your debts for years to come.) The estate is then considered "closed out." All this takes anywhere from four months to a year. If you have prepared properly, chosen an executor and an attorney, things usually go fairly quickly.

What Steps Do I Take?

The first step in drafting your will is to inventory your property. Make a list of all significant items you own. Are there special items that you have specific instructions for? Maybe you have a gold ring that you want to leave to a daughter, or a coin or baseball card collection that you want your son to have. Either put this in writing in your will or talk with your family to make sure everyone agrees on who will receive what. Identify "real property" (i.e., land, houses or other real estate that you own). Identify other assets, such as bank accounts, stocks, mutual funds, certificates of deposit, individual retirement accounts, life insurance and so on. Some of you may own your own business, and you should get your business valued.

Having done all that, you will be able to estimate the net value of the estate. A word of warning here: If you are including the purchase price of your home in your calculations, bear in mind that unless your mortgage is fully paid off, the bank still owns part of your house. If you bought the house fairly recently, it owns almost all of it.

Now you are ready to decide who will get what. In some cases, there may be an individual or individuals that you want to disinherit. I was involved with one case involving an older woman with an estranged husband whom she had not seen in twenty years. She did not want him to show up and claim her estate, so in her will she expressly stated that he was to receive nothing. Remember to carefully express your wishes with respect to guardianship of your children. Also, name alternative recipients for gifts. People you have left things to may themselves pass away, so it is a good idea to have another person listed to receive the gift.

Choosing an Executor

The final task in drawing up a will is to name an executor. This, above all, should be someone you trust, someone who knows you, someone who has your best interests at heart and someone who will take care to do everything exactly the way you want it done. Where possible, it is also a good idea to choose someone with good financial and organizational skills. You can specify that they need to serve with bond, which is a legal term meaning that you are requiring them to purchase insurance in the event that they mismanage your estate. Executors are entitled to a fee. You do not *have* to pay them one; it is entirely a personal decision.

If possible, choose an executor who lives in the same state. Crossing state lines can complicate matters and slow down the process of closing out your estate. Obviously, your executor should be someone whom you are reasonably confident will survive you. Naming your 98-year-old great-aunt Matilda may not be the smartest move. If you choose, your spouse can be your executor. Personally, I did not choose my wife as my executor, because if something were ever to happen to me, I know that the last thing she would want is to have to deal with the financial and legal details of my estate. Some people, on the other hand, find this kind of work therapeutic. This is a personal decision you should make after much discussion and reflection.

Naturally, you should inform your executor that you would like them to serve in this capacity. Don't let them be put off by the title "executor." It sounds intimidating, but there is really very little to it. Basically all they are required to do is to contact an attorney to have them take care of the legal details. They are what I term "the gentle, persuasive nag," nagging the attorney to get him or her to take care of everything promptly.

Guardianship of Your Children

Even if you get nothing else from this chapter, please pay attention here. When we are talking about the guardianship of your children, we are dealing with nothing less than your children's salvation—not what kind of house they will be raised in, what kind of opportunities they will have, or anything else. Ultimately, what I want is to have my children in heaven with me. I hope they have a great life here on earth, but I would much rather that they have deprivation and hardship and make it to heaven than have a perfect life and not make it. This is my deep conviction.

Certainly, you do not want to leave your children with just anyone, not even just anyone in the church. Think carefully about this issue. Get advice and pray over it. For the most part, of course, the church is far better than anything else, but there are situations that are not ideal.

Once you have made your decision, there is, however, something important you must understand: The court does not need to abide by your wishes. While this is a scary thought, keep two things in mind. First, most judges and most courts try to do what is right. Second, there are additional measures you can take to try to ensure that a couple from your church raises your children. You can specifically state in your will *why* this is your wish. In your statement, be detailed. Give specific reasons, such as their child-rearing abilities, their strong faith, their good marriage. Make it clear to the court that you have thought long and hard about the subject. Your message will go a long way toward winning the judge over.

> *"No eye has seen,*
> *no ear has heard,*
> *no mind has conceived*
> *what God has prepared for those who love him."*
> *(1 Corinthians 2:9)*

Because you love your family even as God loves his family, be sure that you prepare things for those you love and those who love you. If you do not have a will, begin work on it today! Remember, God went to great lengths to provide for you, and you should do likewise for the ones you love.

Buying Your
First Home

BY JOHN HANES & MICHAEL DiCHIARO

Disciples often ask: If I have the money or I can get the money, should I use it to buy a home? If I do, am I being a good steward and a wise disciple, or am I being selfish and materialistic? A spiritual question deserves a spiritual answer, and God gives us one in Deuteronomy 8:

> *When you have eaten and are satisfied, praise the Lord for the good land he has given you. Be careful that you do not forget the Lord your God, failing to observe his commands, his laws and his decrees that I am giving you this day. Otherwise, when you eat and are satisfied, when you build fine houses and settle down, and when your herds and flocks grow large and your silver and gold increase and all you have is multiplied, then your heart will become proud and you will forget the Lord your God, who brought you out of Egypt, out of the land of slavery....*
>
> *But remember the Lord your God, for it is he who gives you the ability to produce wealth, and so confirms his covenant, which he swore to your forefathers, as it is today. (Deuteronomy 8:10-14, 18)*

God says if you are going to buy a house, then do it for him. Do it remembering him, and do it with the intention of serving him with your house. Jesus said that we should use our wealth to win friends in this world:

> *"I tell you, use worldly wealth to win friends for yourselves, so that when it is gone, you will be welcomed into eternal dwellings." (Luke 16:9)*

While Jesus did not intend for this statement to answer the question of whether we should or should not buy a house, he certainly intended the principle to apply if we do. Furthermore, the Bible commands us to be hospitable and entertain strangers (presumably, in our homes):

> *Do not forget to entertain strangers, for by so doing some people have entertained angels without knowing it. (Hebrews 13:2)*

Think and pray about your decision. Ask yourself how you can use your home for the kingdom. Let your desire to serve others influence the type of house you buy and where you buy it. Remember, the house is not being purchased just to meet your needs: "Unless the LORD builds the house, its builders labor in vain" (Psalm 127:1a). Likewise, Jesus encourages us to sit down and count the cost before we begin to build:

> *"Suppose one of you wants to build a tower. Will he not first sit down and estimate the cost to see if he has enough money to complete it? For if he lays the foundation and is not able to finish it, everyone who sees it will ridicule him, saying, 'This fellow began to build and was not able to finish.'" (Luke 14:28-30)*

If you enter into the business of buying a house with an unspiritual mindset, the work, time and pressure involved will take its toll on you, your marriage, your discipleship and your walk with God. There is plenty of pressure involved! You may find a house that is your dream home and be certain that this is the house God has planned for you, and then another buyer may outbid you. If you have not resolved in your heart to trust God and give it all to him, you may become embittered. Do not rush! Trust God's timing. If you are meant to have a particular house, no one is going to take it away from you. If you are not meant to have it, no amount of stress and worry is going to change the fact.

If you do have the kind of spiritual mindset God expects, the stress of finding and buying a home will be greatly alleviated. The principles and guidelines in this chapter are intended to be a practical guide to home buying, but they will be of little use to you if you have not given everything over to God first.

In this chapter, we are assuming that you will be taking out a loan to pay for your house. (If you should be in the unusual position of being able to pay cash, just skip this chapter and go back to the one on investments!) Second, we are assuming that you have manageable debt and are clear of consumer and credit card debt. Last, we are assuming that you have your monthly budget under control and know how much you have available to make a monthly mortgage payment. That said, let's begin.

Should I Buy a Home?

From the outset, let us urge you to be thorough and cautious as you embark on the tricky and often frustrating business of buying a home. Many times people come to us having already taken a couple of steps toward buying a home that make for future complications. Our hope is that this section will be able to alert you to these complications and make the purchase of your first home as smooth as possible.

As with any major decision, there are pros and cons to buying a home. One major advantage is that you can take a tax deduction on the interest you pay on your mortgage. This is a big consideration, especially in the earlier years of repayment, when by far the largest part of your mortgage payments go toward paying off the interest on the loan.

Another major benefit is building equity. "Equity" is what you put into your home. Interest payments on your mortgage are not equity. Only payments on the principal, the sum of money you borrowed from your lender in order to purchase the house, are considered equity (along with whatever down payment you may have made). At a later time if you were to apply for a home equity loan, you would only be able to borrow against the equity you have put into your home, not on the amount you paid for the house.

You can also increase your equity with a larger down payment, which is discussed in detail later, or by paying off some or all of the mortgage principal. If, for instance, you were to receive an inheritance, you could choose to use some or all of that money to pay off the mortgage. Another way to build equity is by making additions and/or improvements that increase the value of your home. This is sometimes referred to as "sweat equity." Your equity in the house can also increase if property values in your area go up. This is, of course, dependent upon factors more or less outside of your control.

Another asset to owning a home is pride of ownership. It is your domain, yours to do with as you see fit. You are also free to donate the house to a charity later in life, or to leave it to others as part of your estate, assuming the mortgage is paid off.

On the negative side, buying and owning a home is expensive, complicated and time consuming. If the home begins to have problems, like a leaky roof or faulty wiring, you cannot just call the landlord and have him take care of it, like you do when you are renting. It has become your own problem. In addition, there are many up-front costs in buying a home. Last but not least, your monthly mortgage payments will probably be more than what you are currently paying in rent.

Can I Afford It?

Let's assume your desire to buy a home is high and you have found reasonable property that you want to consider. It's worth repeating Luke 14:28 at this point:

> *"Suppose one of you wants to build a tower. Will he not first sit down and estimate the cost to see if he has enough money to complete it? For if he lays the foundation and is not able to finish it, everyone who sees it will ridicule him, saying, 'This fellow began to build and was not able to finish.'"*

Whether you have in mind a new construction, a resale property, a condominium or co-op, Jesus' admonition to count the cost is especially applicable. The first and foremost step in buying a house is to figure out whether it is economically prudent or not. Lending institutions have some general rules of thumb to determine whether or not they will lend you money. These rules are not carved in stone, but for the most part, they hold true. Generally, a bank will not loan you money unless the total of all your existing monthly debt payments (e.g. credit card payments, car payments, school loan payments, personal loan payments) plus the contemplated monthly housing-related payments (i.e. mortgage, property taxes, school taxes, hazard insurance) is less than or equal to 38 percent of your gross monthly income. Additionally, the contemplated monthly housing-related payments must be less than or equal to 32 percent of your gross monthly income. Generally, both of these rules must be true for the bank to lend you money. Other banks may apply higher percentages (i.e. 48 percent and 42 percent, respectively) but not surprisingly, these loans usually have higher interest rates.

While there are other factors that lending institutions will take into account, these are good rules of thumb to help you determine whether buying a house is wise for you now. Also, bear in mind that even if a bank is willing to lend you money to buy a home, it does not necessarily mean that buying a home is the best decision for you at this time. Remember, owning a home limits your other options in life. Do you want to spend almost a third of your income on a mortgage payment? For example, if you buy a house and subsequently decide that you would like to further your education, you may not be able to. The overall key is to think and plan carefully and spiritually.

Where Do I Go for a Loan?

Several different lender options are available, and some of these are listed here.

Mortgage Broker

A mortgage broker does not lend money. Their job is to shop around, locate funds for you, and put together the most attractive mortgage package that they can. In our experience of working with mortgage brokers, we have found that, as in most fields, there are good ones and bad ones. Some genuinely work hard for their customers, providing very good service and especially helping people with serious credit problems. Others are, to put it charitably, less than straightforward and honest. Broker's fees are not regulated, which means that brokers can charge whatever they want, as long as they disclose it. I have seen brokers charge fees as high as 12 percent of the mortgage amount in an up-front fee (a commission paid directly by you!) and the back-end fee (a premium paid by the bank to the broker). If you have no experience, you may find yourself agreeing to these kinds of unconscionable rates because you do not know any better or you fail to read the fine print. *Do your homework* and get referrals from people you know and trust. By the time a lawyer gets involved in the home-buying process, you will already have signed an unbreakable agreement with your broker.

Another way that mortgage brokers can make money is by essentially cutting a deal with the bank. A typical scenario is as follows: Suppose you have some credit problems, and the bank offers the broker a mortgage at 10 percent for you, which is about two and a half points above the going rate right now. The broker might say to the bank, "No, let's charge them 11 percent, and if I can get them to sign a deal at that price, how much will you pay me as a premium for bringing you a profitable loan?" The broker will tell you not to worry about this fee because the bank is paying it. Yet, you are ultimately going to pay in the form of a higher interest rate.

It all boils down to being careful: Find a broker who has a solid reputation. Know every in and out of the deal you are agreeing to before you sign anything. Read the documents; ask the questions. If the broker responds to your queries with defensiveness, vagueness or an unwillingness to put the agreements in writing, walk out. This is your prerogative.

CREDIT UNIONS

Some credit unions are only open to employees of a particular firm or organization; others accept walk-ins. They are generally smaller and easier to work with than banks.

BANKS

Banks are major financial institutions such as Citibank and Chase Manhattan. This type of institution typically will only work with people who have absolutely no credit problems. They are generally a good source but perhaps not the best choice for everyone.

MORTGAGE BANKS

Mortgage banks are similar to institutional banks, but they deal exclusively with mortgages and do not provide any other services. They are a good source, even though they ordinarily do not service mortgages themselves: Immediately after closing, most of them sell the mortgage to someone in the secondary market, which is how they make their money. Generally, your loan ends up with a reputable lending institution that will provide you good service.

RETIREMENT ACCOUNTS/IRAS

If you have enough money in your company retirement account—your 401(k)—or independent retirement account (IRA), you can choose to borrow against it to finance a mortgage.

Whichever route you choose to take, use personal referrals to seek out reputable brokers, banks and lending institutions. Don't just pick a name out of the phone book. The market for mortgages is often very competitive so you may be able to negotiate lower bank fees or even have them waived.

A bank will often agree to lower the lending rate if you pay points on a loan up front. A "point" is simply one percent of the mortgage and is considered prepaid interest, which is generally immediately deductible on your tax return for the year that it is paid (please consult with your accountant). For example, let's say a bank agrees to lower your interest rate by one percent if you pay three points on a $100,000 loan. Three percent of $100,000 is $3,000, but it will save you $1,000 per year. In three years, you will break even and thereafter will continue to save $1,000 per year for the remainder of the loan.

As you enter the realm of home buying, bear in mind that there are ways to dramatically reduce the amount of interest paid over the course of a 30-year mortgage. For example you can make an extra payment every year that is specifically earmarked to pay off the principal. You can also make biweekly as opposed to monthly payments if your promissory note allows. Inquire with your accountant, financial advisor or mortgage consultant for further details.

Total Price of Owning a Home

The chart below breaks down, as exhaustively as possible, the different costs and fees involved in owning a home.

FEE DESCRIPTION	AMOUNT ($)
Engineering inspection	250 to 500
Termite inspection	80 to 120
Attorney's fees	850 to 2000
Bank appraisal	250 to 350
Bank application fees	200 to 400
Bank nonrefundable fee (e.g. rate lock-in)	½% to 2% of loan amount
Hazard insurance premium (one year)	500 to 2000
Cost of property	
Down payment (upon signing contract)	10% of purchase price
Remainder of payment (by you)	10% unless there's PMI
	(premium mortgage insurance)
Balance of payment	(your lender pays this)
Closing costs	
Miscellaneous credits to seller	
• Prorated share of property tax	Depends on tax and timing
• Prorated share of school tax	Depends on tax and timing
• Oil left in oil tank	Varies
• Water meter	Varies
• Additional adjustments	Varies

FEE DESCRIPTION	AMOUNT ($)
Closing Costs (con't.)	
Recording costs	100 to 300
Mortgage recording tax	_% of mortgage minus $25 (varies)
Title search costs	400 to 600
Title insurance	1000 to 4000
Survey (updated vs. new)	250 to 1000
Bank attorneys	400 to 850
Bank escrow for taxes/hazard insurance	varies—may not be required
Short term interest on mortgage	varies—depends on day of month
Additional bank closing fees	400 to 600
Gratuity to title closer	50 to 75 per hour

Starting the Process

When you have found a home you are interested in, typically the practice is to have an engineering inspection done at that point, before any contract is signed. This does not mean you are obligated to buy the property or conversely, that the seller must sell the house to you. Engineering inspections are typically done first so that, from the buyer's perspective, you can decide to pull out if the inspection and evaluation of the house is unsatisfactory or so that you can either negotiate a price reduction or the making of repairs. Get a referral from someone who has used the engineer previously and was satisfied with the job he did. Make sure the engineer is licensed. An inspection normally takes about two hours and the engineer is looking for major structural and design problems (e.g., roof, asbestos, foundation, wiring, etc.). He should also test for radon. If your water is supplied by a well, the well should also be tested, as should your septic field if you have a septic tank sewage system. If you are worried about lead paint, have the paint tested. It is also important that the engineer inspects for termites. Termite problems are not covered in hazard insurance, which is the general policy that covers you against fire and other perils.

If you are at all serious about the property, you should definitely have the inspection done. In most states, the rule is "caveat emptor" (buyer beware). In other words the burden is on you, the buyer, to find out what problems the house may have. Generally speaking, the owner will not bring them to your attention.

If possible, you should plan to accompany the engineer when he or she makes the inspection, as it is a great way to learn about the home you are thinking of purchasing. What you need to be concerned about are major structural problems, such as a roof that will need replacing, a sagging foundation or termites. These types of serious problems can either be factored into the overall deal you make for purchasing the house, or you can decide against buying it altogether. More minor things, such as a heating system that needs to be repaired or a missing doorknob, will be your responsibility, unless there is a very strong buyer's market at your time of purchase. Also note that if you separately purchase any furnishings or equipment from the homeowner, you should inform your attorney. This is because you will have to pay sales tax on them unless, as is customary, an agreement is made that these items are being transferred free along with the house as part of the deal.

Keeping a written expense log listing every expenditure you make in purchasing your home is an excellent idea. Every time you write a check or pay for anything for the house, great or small, enter the amount in your log. In this way you will be better equipped to understand the numbers when your lawyer presents you with a summary of all expenses made.

Many costs on the Fee Description List vary greatly. Keeping costs to a minimum is not harmful, but bear in mind that you usually get what you pay for.

Using a Real Estate Agent

Some houses are for sale by owner, which generally means getting a property for less because you can cut out the real estate agent's fees. In most cases, however, you will probably work with a real estate agent to find the home you want. Real estate agents, like most people, work to their own advantage. Unless they are being hired exclusively by you (in which case they are known as a "buyer's broker"), and you have a written contract that they are exclusively a buyer's agent, you can assume that they are working for the seller. As such, their job is to increase the price of the property you are interested in to as high as the market will stand. They will probably show you properties in a higher price range than you have indicated, and in some cases will show you only properties listed by their agency (so that they do not have to split the commission with anyone else). This is not to say they are not fine people, but remember that no matter how friendly and agreeable they may be, they work for the seller—not for you.

Factors Affecting Home Cost

What factors determine the price of a home? Our answer starts with the three most important words in real estate: location, location, location. The New York metropolitan area, for example, is extremely expensive because the general desire to live near the city drives prices up. If the property is in the suburbs of a major city, the ease of the commute affects price. How close a house is to the street, to a power plant or to a school all make a difference. The quality of the school district that the house is located in has a significant effect on cost also. The type of neighborhood the house is located in is another factor. The general availability of vacant lots and the amount of houses currently for sale in an area are other factors. For example, if the area is overdeveloped and houses are sold as soon as they are placed on the market, then prices will be high. Finally, the size of the house itself and the amount of land the house is situated on have a great bearing on price. Have your real estate agent give you a Comparative Market Analysis (also called a CMA), which provides a sample of the recent sale prices in an area, to help you decide where you want to live. Some factors will be more important to you than others. If you work at home, for instance, the ease of commute will be less important to you.

Allowing Time

Note the most important caution we can offer as you buy your first home: *Do not become emotional about a piece of property.* It is extremely easy to do this, especially if it is a house you really like. If you do become emotional, we guarantee that you will spend more money than you should and will otherwise make many mistakes. If you are in a rush, and the agent knows you are in a rush, he or she may try to get you to purchase *any* property.

Be content to take your time. It may take months to find what you want, but you will eventually find a suitable property and, once comfortably installed, you will be very grateful that you decided to be patient. Remember, the house you think is just the right one for you may be bought by someone who puts in a higher bid than you did. Also, it may take you some time to decide where you want to live. You may eventually decide to build your own house. The unexpected is the norm, so be prepared to take things slowly.

Building a House

There are pros and cons to building your own home. On the plus side, building a home allows you to customize it to your taste and lifestyle. Do you want a walk-in closet for the master bedroom, or a den where you can house your CD collection? You can build those in if you want. In certain states you will also get a warranty with your new home, guaranteeing the quality of construction. Finally, there should be fewer repairs—and head-aches—with a new house.

On the minus side, building your own home is usually more expensive than purchasing a resale property. You and your law-yer will have to work with a builder, who is more savvy than the average homeowner. You will have to spend a lot of time on specifications for the home. Landscaping, which you will need to do yourself after the house is completed, can be costly and time-consuming. A new yard takes time to mature; be prepared to have a sparse lawn for a few years! Finally, you cannot see the house you are buying until after it has been built. The bottom line, again, is deciding what is most important and feasible for you and making a decision accordingly.

Co-ops and Condominiums

A co-op is a corporation that you become part of if you buy an apartment in a building owned by the corporation. You do not own the apartment you buy; you own shares of stock in the corporation. You do not receive a deed, but what is known as a "proprietary lease," in which the buyer is the tenant and the co-op is the landlord. Furthermore, you cannot become part of the co-op until the co-op board, which typically has restrictive and sometimes rather arbitrary guidelines for admission, approves you. You will have to submit a lengthy application form to the board, as well as documents outlining your complete financial status. The board can reject you for any reason and is not re-quired to give you an explanation.

If you are approved, you probably will not be able to sublet your apartment. If you are permitted, it will be for a year or two at most and you may have to pay a fee to the co-op to do so. There is usually an underlying mortgage on the building that your apartment is situated in, so you are not only paying your mortgage, you are also paying high maintenance costs to cover the building's mortgage. In addition, you are paying for the repairs, maintenance and real estate taxes associated with the building. In short, we do not recommend a co-op if you can avoid it. If you do decide to buy one, however, here are some questions you should ask your realtor to get answers for:

Ask for a copy of the building's financial records for the last two years. If the co-op is financially unhealthy and goes belly-up, you will go belly-up with it.

If the building has an underlying mortgage, find out how large it is and what percentage of your mortgage is devoted to paying it.

Find out what maintenance payment increases have occurred over the last five years.

Find out if the building has had any special assessments over the last five years.

On the plus side with co-ops, you will not need a termite inspection. (You can, however, have an engineering inspection done if you want to.) You will not need title insurance or a survey. You will not have to pay a mortgage recording tax, although you will have to pay a transfer agent fee.

The picture is rather brighter with condominiums. Condos also have a board of directors, but they do not have as much power as a co-op board. Owners typically have more flexibility when it comes to subletting. Also, you own the townhouse or apartment, rather than owning shares in a corporation. You also own a share of the common areas in the apartment complex (lobby, pool, grounds, etc.) relative to the size of your apartment.

Making an Offer

Before you make an offer on a property, however, do your homework. The more information you have about the property and the neighborhood it is located in, the better your position in negotiating. Talk to the homeowner and to the neighbors. Find out what appliances, if any, the owner intends to leave behind and how old they are. Get a recent repair history: When was the roof replaced? Has the basement ever flooded? Is it damp? What major repairs, if any, has the owner done during his or her time in the house? What extra expenses could you expect after moving in?

Another source for information is the county clerk's office. There you can look up records and see how many past owners there have been. If you find out that past owners have typically only stayed a few years each, ask yourself why. If, on the other hand, people have tended to live in the house for twenty or thirty years at a time, that may indicate a wise purchase. You can also use the county clerk's office to find out how much the current owner paid for the house. Bear in mind, of course, that that value will probably have increased since then, and certainly the price will be higher in a seller's market.

Finally, talk to the neighbors and find out about the area. Is it generally safe? What are the schools like? If you have school-age children, make an appointment to visit the schools to see what they are like. You should also ask your broker to give you a Comparative Market Analysis (CMA) to see recent sale prices of houses similar to the one you are considering purchasing.

The amount of negotiating room for a purchase price is largely dependent on market forces outside your control. In a seller's market, other people may bid for the same property at or above the asking price. In general, though, the final price tends to be midway between the owner's asking price and your first offer. If you are a good negotiator, you may do better than that. Ultimately, as with everything else, you must pray and trust that if God wants you to have the house, you will have it.

Finding a Lawyer to Start the Contract

Your next step is to find a lawyer whom you trust so you can start putting together a contract. Attorneys' fees can vary according to whether you are buying a house, a co-op or a condo. As mentioned earlier, bear in mind that you will get what you pay for.

The relationship between you and the lawyer is one based on service. You are paying him (or her) to write the contract the way you want it written and to negotiate for what you want. Your lawyer, however, cannot read your mind; you must be specific about what you want—don't make assumptions. In addition, your lawyer does not have all the answers but has opinions (limited by experience).

The seller's lawyer prepares the contract, and you and your lawyer review it. You must read the contract personally. Yes, it is boring and dense, but you must read it, and read it carefully. Make a list of items you do not understand, and ask questions until you do. The contract is usually a standard form document, with both sides adding "riders" (i.e. additional provisions) to tailor the contract to the specific needs of a particular deal. You should definitely add a rider that lists the appliances that are to be included in the sale and obtain a guarantee that they are in good working order on the day of closing. In addition, you should try to obtain guarantees that the plumbing and electrical systems are in good working order and that the roof is free of leaks.

This does not mean that they are in pristine or perfect condition but that they are in working order.

From the buyer's perspective, the most crucial term is the Mortgage Contingency Clause. This essentially says to the buyer, "I want to buy your house, but it's contingent on my getting a mortgage. If I can't get a mortgage from the bank, I can't buy the house and I can legally pull out of the deal and get my down payment back." The standard contract (without the Mortgage Contingency Clause) does not supply enough protection to buyers if difficulties arise.

Other issues to discuss with your attorney would be a Notices Clause and the type of deed you will be receiving. Those are important issues that we cannot go into here.

If many other buyers are bidding on the house you are interested in, then talk to your lawyer and agent to make sure the seller's lawyer is moving on your contract. You should also make sure that your own lawyer is reviewing the contract in a timely manner. However, you should allow a lot of time in the contract so you don't have to rush things unduly. You have to allow time for your bank to make a decision on approving your loan (typically 35-45 days after the contract is signed), time for your title search company to do a title search (up to three weeks from the time your loan comes in), and time to get out of your current rental situation, assuming you are in one. When does your lease expire? Where will you live if the house isn't ready? What are the penalties for breaking your lease? Can you pay on a month-to-month basis?

Be aware that the closing date listed in the contract, which is the date on which the deal is finalized and the money changes hands, is an approximate date only (with some rare exceptions).

When the deal is closed, it is not uncommon for the seller to ask to remain in the house for a week or more after he has transferred the deed to you. Avoid this type of situation at all costs: It may lead you to a landlord-tenant court trying to get someone out of your house. Also, if you are ready to move in and the seller is not ready to move out, you can lose your bank commitment, which is only good for a certain period of time. After that date you have to pay extra fees to extend the bank commitment. You also run the risk of not getting your commitment extended if your circumstances change. For example, you may lose your job—of course in that case, you are probably better off not buying!

Down Payments

A down payment is the amount of money that you personally are putting toward the cost of the property. This amount is not covered by the mortgage. Typically, the down payment consists of paying 10 percent of the purchase price upon signing the contract and another 10 percent upon closing, totaling 20 percent. You will also have to pay closing costs, unless these are figured into your monthly mortgage payment, which can be done. It is possible to negotiate the amount of the down payment and pay an amount equaling 15 percent, rather than 20. The down side is that if you put less than 20 percent down, your bank will make you pay for PMI, which ensures them full payment should you default on the loan. From your bank's perspective, the more of your own money you have put into the house, the more likely you are to be careful not to lose it.

Before Signing the Contract

The engineering inspection and report needs to be completed before you sign the contract. Read the report yourself before signing the contract and discuss it with your engineer and your lawyer. If anything is not up to code, ask the seller to fix it.

Review the inspection contract and make sure you are covered if the engineer misses something. Tour the house yourself at least once or twice. Visit on a rainy day to see if the basement or roof leaks. Learn how to use complicated appliances or devices (pool, Jacuzzi, etc.). Generally, you are expected to do a walk-through of the house either the day before or the day of closing to ensure that the house is in good shape and is in the same condition as when you signed the contract. If there are new or unexpected problems with the house, you might be able to negotiate a reduction in price or you may have to delay the closing to give the seller time to fix the problem.

After Signing the Contract

After you have signed on the dotted line, everyone will be working toward closing the transaction. Be sure to follow up with your attorney to make sure he is expediting the closing process as much as possible. He or she is probably working on twenty other projects at the same time and may leave things until the last minute. The squeaky wheel, as they say, gets the oil. Also, follow up with your real estate agent. He or she should be contacting all parties to facilitate the process. Make sure that your attorney asks the seller's attorney to contact the seller's bank to obtain a bank payoff letter. This letter is from the seller's bank specifying the balance of his existing mortgage on the house, if one exists, which he must pay in full before selling to you. If the seller's attorney does not do this, the seller will not be ready to close when you are.

What Happens at Closing

Just prior to closing, usually a day or two before, you need to do a final walk-through of the property in order to ensure that appliances work, there is no damage, required items were fixed and the property is in more or less the same condition it was in when you had the inspection performed. Once you get to the closing table, be ready to sign lots of papers. Your lawyer should briefly explain them to you, but no changes are permitted at this point, other than incorrect spellings, mistakes in interest rates, and so forth. The certified checks that your lawyer should have obtained for you are now distributed to the seller to pay for the house, and the seller in turn presents you with the deed to the house. The deed legally certifies that you are the new owner of the property.

Checks are also delivered to the title company to pay various charges. Talk with your lawyer in advance and decide how the title will be taken (i.e., how the property will be owned). There are several options.

The seller hands over all keys and the garage door opener, where applicable. Also be sure to get instruction manuals for all appliances and any warranties for same. You are now the proud owner of your first home!

Further Resources

We realize that this is a huge amount of information to digest all at once, but do not let it discourage you. No one finds first-time home buying easy, and the process is less than user-friendly. Be patient, seek plenty of advice (particularly from other disciples who have been down this road before), move slowly and carefully, and above all, trust God, and you will be fine. We have listed some further resources below to help you on your way.

You can get the booklet "Buying Your Home," published by the US Department of Housing and Urban Development, online at www.hud.gov. Any mortgage broker or bank offering you a loan is required by law to give you a copy. Obtaining and reading this booklet before you take any steps toward buying a home is best. In addition, ask your mortgage broker about other booklets. They are available on a wide variety of topics, including understanding adjustable rate vs. fixed rate mortgages.

Booklets from the Environmental Protection Agency (EPA) on Lead Paint and Radon are available at www.epa.gov. Find your local EPA office through directory assistance.

For information about loans and finances, try www.quicken.com.

Life Insurance

Life insurance provides dollars to a beneficiary when an insured dies. The money that becomes available provides the resources to carry on a lifestyle, to pay off a mortgage, to make available funds for college and to provide for a transition. In general, you may need five times your annual net income, plus an amount to pay off a home mortgage, debt and enough to establish or contribute to a college fund. Ask yourself these questions, starting with, "If I had died last night..." How much money would it take to pay off my mortgage, establish a college education fund and provide a capital amount to fund the family's monthly budget? (Take into consideration inflation.) Be careful not to judge incorrectly what is "a lot" of money. To make provision for a family in the event of a death may take more money than you think.

For example when a father dies and the mother has been staying home with young children, the family faces the possibility of mom needing to work outside the home in order to take on the financial responsibilities of providing for the family. This raises the issue of needing to fund daycare for the children as well. Challenging questions must be answered if the funds are not there to enable the family to continue living as they are accustomed. Does the church become the provider for the family? Does the family rely on or move in with grandparents? Adequate provision may allow a family to continue in their current ministry, friendships and discipling relationships. Adequate provision may make the difference in being faithful to God, thus Paul's admonition in 1 Timothy 5:8.

There are different kinds of life insurance. Goals and objectives will determine the type you consider. There are policies for personal needs, business needs, estate planning and selective benefits for tax planning. Level-term policies from high quality insurers have never been cheaper. Adequate protection is available for a very reasonable cost. Seek advice from a professional, and you will make a good decision.

APPENDIX 2

Detailed Budget Worksheet

Budget Form						
	Wkly		Monthly		Annual	
Income						
Source A_____						
Source B_____						
Source C_____						
TOTAL INCOME						
Contribution						
Benevolence Contribution						
Orphan Contribution						
Church Related (BTs, etc)						
Special Contribution						
House (Rent/Mortgage)						
Electric						
Water						
Snow Removal, Lawn Care						
Appliances and Furniture						
Home Maintenance						
Natural Gas/Oil						
Trash Removal						
Food						
Cosmetics, Paper, Cleaners, etc						
Clothing						
Birthday Gifts						
Christmas Gifts						
Friends Gifts						
Auto Payment						
Auto Insurance						
Auto Gas						
Auto Maintenance						
Telephone						
Eating Out						
Entertainment						
Haircuts						
Pet Care						
Life Insurance						
Family Trips						
Marriage Get-a-Ways						
Vacation						
Medical						
Newspaper/Magazines						
TV Cable						
Debt Service						
Other _____						
Other _____						
Other _____						
Other _____						
Other _____						
TOTAL EXPENSES						
NET (INCOME LESS EXPENSES)						

Permission is granted to photocopy this form.

Contributors

DANIEL H. BATHON, JR.

Dan graduated from Villanova University with a degree in business administration. From 1983 to 1989 he was Vice President and then Senior Vice President and partner with the Wall Street firm of Drexel Burnham Lambert. While he was with Drexel he raised $500 million for the Chrysler Finance Corporation and brought Warner Communication back into the commercial paper market, eventually issuing over $500 million in short-term notes on Warner's behalf. In 1989 while on the mission team to Paris, Dan left Drexel and began his own European investment banking company.

In 1989 he returned to the United States where he has helped begin several new companies. Since 1990 he has served as the World Sector Administrator for the New England/Europe World Sector of the International Churches of Christ. He and his wife, Julie, have three children, D.H. (15), Grace (13) and Alexandra (10).

JOHN BRINGARDNER

John earned a Juris Doctor from Florida State University and for the following six years, he served as a trial lawyer in Tallahassee, Florida. In 1987 he gave up his law career and moved his family to Boston where he and his wife, Emily, joined the ministry staff. John and Emily were asked to move to Bangkok, Thailand, where they planted the pillar church for Southeast Asia in 1990. They led the church in Bangkok for two years and then moved to lead the church in Manila for one year.

In 1993 John and his family moved to Los Angeles to help start the Media/Law World Sector of the International Churches of Christ (ICC). He passed the California Bar in 1994 and now serves as General Counsel of the ICC and World Sector Administrator of the Media/Law World Sector. He and Emily also serve as a congregational deacon and deaconess for the Los Angeles International Church of Christ.

John and Emily have two sons, J.T. (14) and Michael (12), and one daughter, Malee (10).

STEVE JOHNSON

Steve Johnson is the lead evangelist for the New York City Church of Christ and the World Sector Leader for the ACES World Sector, and along with his wife, Lisa, oversees churches in Africa, the Caribbean, New York and several other eastern seaboard states. The seminar featuring the writers of this volume and the book that grew out of that seminar were both ideas Steve conceived to serve first the New York City Church and then those in other churches in the kingdom. They have two daughters, McCall (10) and Skylar (6).

JIM BROWN

Jim and his wife Teresa are on the ministry staff of the New York Church of Christ, and they oversee various ministries in New York state. Jim was a missionary to Brazil for many years. Currently he and his wife have two children, Mackenzie (4) and Dylan (2).

MADALINE M. EVANS

Madaline M. Evans graduated from Franklin & Marshall College in Lancaster, Pennsylvania, with a bachelor's degree in accounting and is a CPA in New Jersey and Pennsylvania. She has more than 22 years of experience in auditing, accounting and finance, working for such firms as Price Waterhouse, Hoffman LaRoche, ITT–Defense Space Communications, and New Jersey Transit.

After her third year as a disciple (and while a single mom of two teenage boys, Michael and Ronald!), Madaline was asked to work for the New York City Church of Christ. Using her many talents to serve God, she is currently the Assistant Executive Director and Controller for the New York City Church of Christ. She serves on the Board of Directors for the New York City Church of Christ and the ACES World Sector.

Madaline authored several chapters of DPI's *Undivided Devotion*, is featured on DPI's audio set *Working 9 to 5* and speaks to numerous professional and educational institutions throughout New Jersey.

ROBERT GAUNTT

Robert Gauntt grew up in Ft. Worth, Texas, and holds both undergraduate and graduate (MBA) degrees from the University of Texas schools of business, majoring in finance and minoring in real estate and accounting. He worked in New York City for three years for PaineWebber and then for Goldman Sachs. He lived in London for a short period.

After having become disciples, Robert and his wife moved to Houston in 1991 where he is now a principal in a premier investment banking firm.

The Gauntts have three boys, Travis (7), Tyler (5) and Turner (4 months).

JOHN W. HANES

John W. Hanes graduated from Princeton University in 1987 with a bachelor's degree in operations research engineering (statistical modeling). In October of 1987, John was baptized and became a disciple in the New York City Church of Christ.

John worked first as a programmer for the city of New York and then as a computer consultant for both Smith Barney and Deloitte & Touche. In the fall of 1989, he met his future wife, Vivian Rivera-Hanes. At the time, Vivian had just assumed the lead administrative role in the New York City Church of Christ. Today, she serves as the World Sector Administrator for the Africa/Caribbean/Eastern Seaboard (ACES) World Sector.

In 1993 John attended the Fordham University School of Law. He completed law school in 1996 and successfully passed both the New York and New Jersey bar exams. Since that time he has served as General Counsel for the ACES World Sector of the International Churches of Christ. The Hanes have one son, Wesley.

MICHAEL DICHIARO

Michael DiChiaro received his bachelor's degree from Columbia College in 1984, where he was honored for his stellar performances on and off the baseball field. Following college,

Michael received his jurisprudence doctorate from Fordham University School of Law in 1988.

Michael began his legal career working at a large law firm in New York City. Currently, Michael has his own law firm in Rockland County, New York, which specializes in business litigation, real estate, international law, estates, wills and trusts, and corporate counseling.

He and his wife, Ronda, are members of the New York City Church of Christ. They have two children, Tyler (7) and Mia (5).

GREGORY A. GARCIA

Gregory A. Garcia began his college career as an architecture student but changed majors in the middle of his junior year to accounting. Thoroughly enjoying the law-related classes in his new major, he applied to and later graduated from the University of Georgia Law School in Athens, Georgia.

Upon graduation from law school, he had job offers from five of the "Big Eight" international accounting firms. Since he was fluent in Spanish, they all wanted him in their Miami offices. He took his first job with Deloitte, Haskins & Sells, and later went with Touche Ross & Co. His wife, Kay, worked on the ministry staff of the Miami-Gables Church of Christ. Michael passed the Georgia and Florida bar exams and the CPA exam and was licensed in both professions in both states.

In early 1982, the Garcias desired to relocate to Athens. He began a private law practice with a former law professor of his there.

Gregory and Kay have two adopted children, Aime (14) and Alec (11).

Who Are We?

Discipleship Publications International (DPI) began publishing in 1993. We are a nonprofit Christian publisher committed to publishing and distributing materials that honor God, lift up Jesus Christ and show how his message practically applies to all areas of life. We have a deep conviction that no one changes life like Jesus and that the implementation of his teaching will revolutionize any life, any marriage, any family and any singles household.

Since our beginning we have published more than 75 titles; plus we have produced a number of important, spiritual audio products. More than one million volumes have been printed, and our works have been translated into more than a dozen languages—international is not just a part of our name! Our books are shipped monthly to every inhabited continent.

To see a more detailed description of our works, find us on the World Wide Web at **www.dpibooks.org**. You can order books listed on the following pages by calling 1-888-DPI-BOOK twenty-four hours a day.

We appreciate the hundreds of comments we have received from readers. We would love to hear from you. Here are other ways to get in touch:

Mail: DPI, 2 Sterling Road, Billerica, MA 01862-2595
E-mail: dpibooks@icoc.org

Find us on the
World Wide Web

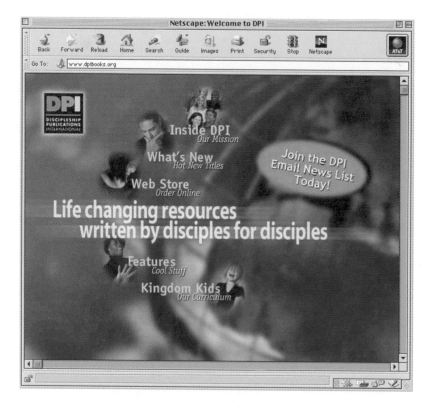

www.dpibooks.org
1-888-DPI-BOOK